Combat Aircraft Library

British and European Combat Aircraft

Combat Aircraft Library

British and European Combat Aircraft

Paul A. Jackson

Crescent Books
New York

Crescent Books

First English edition published by Temple Press
an imprint of Newnes Books 1983

All rights reserved.
This edition published by Crescent Books,
a division of Crown Publishers, Inc.
h g f e d c b a

Printed and bound in Italy

Created and produced by Stan Morse
Aerospace Publishing Ltd
10 Barley Mow Passage
London W4 4PH

© Copyright Aerospace Publishing Ltd 1983

Colour profiles and line diagrams © Pilot Press Ltd

All correspondence concerning the content of this volume should be addressed to Aerospace
Publishing Ltd. Trade enquiries should be addressed to Crescent Books, New York

ISBN: 0-517-405083

Library of Congress Catalog Card Number: 83-70 127

PICTURE ACKNOWLEDGEMENTS
The publishers would like to thank the following people and organisations for their help in
supplying photographs for this book.

Jacket front: Herman Potgieter. **Jacket back:** Saab. **Page 3:** British Aerospace. **6:** British
Aerospace. **7:** MoD. **8:** British Aerospace/MoD. **9:** British Aerospace. **13:** British Aerospace. **14:**
Press Association/COI. **15:** Press Association. **16:** British Aerospace. **17:** British Aerospace. **18:**
Peter Foster. **19:** British Aerospace. **20:** British Aerospace/British Aerospace. **21:** British
Aerospace. **22:** Shorts. **23:** British Aerospace/MoD. **24:** Herman Potgieter. **25:** Herman Potgieter.
27: Lindsay Peacock. **30:** Dassault-Breguet. **32:** Dassault-Breguet. **33:** Dassault-Breguet. **37:**
P. Guerin via EDENA. **38:** Dassault-Breguet/Dassault-Breguet. **39:** Dassault-Breguet. **40:** Herman
Potgieter. **41:** Saab. **42:** Saab/Saab. **43:** Saab. **46:** Saab. **47:** Saab. **48:** SOKO. **49:** Aermacchi. **54:**
Aermacchi. **55:** Aermacchi. **56:** Aeritalia. **57:** CASA. **58:** British Aerospace. **59:** MoD. **62:**
Messerschmitt-Bölkow-Blohm. **64:** Messerschmitt-Bölkow-Blohm. **65:** British Aerospace. **66:**
British Aerospace. **67:** British Aerospace/British Aerospace. **70:** P. Guerin via EDENA. **72:** AIR via
EDENA. **73:** Dassault-Breguet. **77:** Peter Foster. **79:** Aeritalia. **80:** Avions Fairey-SABCA.

Foreword

Without doubt, Europe is, for its size, a prolific source of combat aircraft in numbers of designs, if not always in quantity of their production. Contrasting with the United States and Soviet Union, which select a particular type of aircraft for a specific requirement and then undertake large-scale manufacture both for home use and for their allies, Western Europe has a very different approach to the provision of equipment for its air forces.

Nationalist, neutralist and individualist policies of the various nations have given Europe's air arms a broad selection of locally-built aircraft (plus some imported varieties) with which to undertake their allotted tasks. Wherever possible, however, the major countries endeavour to design and build their own equipment (not least for reasons of prestige), the result being overall duplication of effort amongst nations belonging to the same military alliance, and reduced prospects for export earnings.

In the days when air forces could afford virtually a different aircraft for every purpose this profligacy was accepted, if not encouraged. Now, high development costs force designers to incorporate many diverse capabilities within a single airframe, the consequent larger production runs spreading research costs over a wider field. Even this attempt at economy has proved insufficient with the most advanced combat aircraft and, as will be seen from the final section of this book, the trend in Europe is increasingly towards cost-sharing across international borders.

The UK and France have achieved leadership in the production of indigenous designs for their air arms, although amongst the other European countries Sweden must warrant mention as a producer of first-class aircraft built almost exclusively for local use. NATO members are becoming reliant on licensed production of American aircraft in some instances the principal exceptions in the fixed-wing combat aircraft field being Italy and, to a lesser extent, newly-joined Spain, with West Germany a significant participant in international programmes. Nor must Yugoslavia be forgotten, for as a non-aligned Communist country it produces its own light strike aircraft, as well as importing from East and West.

This book includes the principal European-built combat aircraft in operational service, plus the major prototypes and projects under development. Some fly with only one air force; others are to be seen throughout the world; all testify to the inventiveness and diversity of Europe's aerospace industries.

Contents

British Combat Aircraft

No longer self-sufficient in military aircraft design and manufacture, Britain still has a considerable number of indigenous products in front-line service. Aircraft such as the Harrier, Sea Harrier, Hawk and Strikemaster have achieved widespread export orders.

Shown looping with its two blunt-base drop tanks in place, a British Aerospace Hawk Mk 51 of the Finnish air force is photographed here while on test over the UK and prior to its ferry flight to Helsinki.

An early picture of a Harrier GR.Mk 1 firing 68-mm SNEB rockets against a simulated ground target. Harrier GR.Mk 1s of the RAF have now been modified to GR.Mk 3 standard.

Though the names of pioneer aircraft companies such as Avro, Blackburn, Bristol, de Havilland, English Electric, Hawker, Supermarine and Vickers have now vanished into the anonymity of British Aerospace, their influence lives on in the diverse civilian and military products emanating from the BAe Divisions spread between Surrey and Strathclyde. Of those currently in production, perhaps none has captured the public imagination more than the Harrier and its navalized companion the Sea Harrier, universally and erroneously known as the 'Jump-Jet'.

At the heart of the Harrier's vertical take-off capability lies the unique Bristol Siddeley BS.53 Pegasus engine in which gases, instead of travelling straight through as in conventional jets, are forced out through four swivelling nozzles, enabling the aircraft to rise on a column of gas and then rotate the thrust rearwards for a transition to normal forward flight.

Both engine and airframe were conceived as private ventures (that is, without official support) during the late 1950s, a test aircraft, the Hawker P.1127, flying for the first time on 21 October 1960.

British and European Combat Aircraft

After five more had been built, nine partly militarized variants, known as Kestrels, were used for VTOL feasibility trials by an Anglo-German-US unit based in the UK between October 1964 and November 1965, the intention being that NATO should produce a much more advanced VTOL aircraft by drawing on the lessons learned. The unique tactical advantages of a combat aircraft which could operate independently of vulnerable airfields in time of war was to the forefront of many NATO minds during the 1960s, but for various reasons only the UK saw the project through to fruition.

Financial stringency forced abandonment of the definitive P.1154, projected for both the RAF and Royal Navy, and instead the P.1127 was completely re-engineered as the Harrier. The first of six pre-production Harriers undertook its maiden flight on 31 August 1966, and No. 1 Squadron became the world's first operational VTOL unit when it formed at Wittering on 1 October 1969.

Three squadrons which followed (one has since disbanded) took up station with RAF Germany,

The Falklands campaign again demonstrated the vital need to have aircraft that can operate without airfields. Here Harrier GR.Mk 3 tactical attack and reconnaissance aircraft of No. 1 Sqn, RAF are seen in Arctic camouflage during Exercise 'Cold Winter' in Norway, 1979.

Dispersed in clearings well away from vulnerable airfields, the BAe Harriers of RAF Germany might well be the most important NATO front-line combat aircraft to survive the initial onslaught of a Warsaw Pact offensive into central Europe.

Seen hovering, this VA-1
Matador is no. 4 of the Rota-
based operating squadron Eslla
(Escuadrilla) No. 008, Arma
Aérea de la Armada.

and as the power of the Pegasus was further developed via the Mks 101, 102 and 103, so the aircraft progressed from Harrier GR Mk 1 to 1A and 3, whilst the two-seat trainer version was similarly updated through T.Mks 2, 2A and 4. Even the latest engines were insufficiently powerful to allow vertical take-off with a full weapons load, and thus was developed the STOVL (Short Take-Off, Vertical Landing) technique which can be performed on any strip of road or level grass clearing.

Series production of Harriers for the RAF has totalled 114 single-seaters and 23 trainers, plus four of the latter for the Royal Navy, the principal export order coming from the US Marines for 102 AV-8As and eight TAV-8A trainers, whilst the Spanish navy acquired 13 (including a pair of

The BAe Harrier T.Mk 4A is the
combat readiness trainer
version of the GR.Mk 3, notable
for its additional cockpit and
lack of a laser ranger and
marked-target seeker in the
extreme nose.

British Aerospace Harrier

History and Notes
Hawker Aircraft developed the world's first single-engine jet V/STOL aircraft, the P.1127, in the teeth of official hostility. Thanks to NATO support it flew in 1960, and again thanks to NATO Hawker went ahead on a big supersonic V/STOL combat aircraft, the P.1154, for both the RAF and RN, but this was cancelled by a Labour government. In its place Hawker was allowed to build a small attack aircraft using whatever P.1154 avionics would fit, and the result was the Harrier, in service with the RAF since 1 April 1969. Ultimately the RAF received 114 single-seaters, now all brought up to Harrier GR.Mk 3 standard with laser noses and various ECM fits, plus 21 much longer two-seaters designated Harrier T.Mk 2 or T.Mk 4 with various sub-types. A simple attack version was bought by the US Marine Corps, designated AV-8A (102 plus eight two-seat TAV-8As), which have operated intensively from land or ship bases in close-support missions centred on dive attacks using bombs and rockets. The RAF fly mainly very low-level close-support and interdiction, and since the Falklands war followed the USMC in carrying self-protection Sidewinders. A five-camera reconnaissance pod can be fitted. The Spanish navy bought 11 AV-8As and two TAV-8As for land and sea basing. By 1983 most surviving AV-8As had been reworked to AV-8C standard with 4,000-hour fatigue-free life and completely updated and augmented avionics. The Sea Harrier and AV-8B are described separately.

Specification: British Aerospace Harrier GR.Mk 3
Origin: UK
Type: V/STOL close-support attack and reconnaissance
Armament: two 30-mm Aden cannon each with 130 rounds attached under fuselage; external weapon load of 5,000 lb (2268 kg) or more (up to 8,000 lb/3629 kg has been lifted) comprising tanks, bombs, rocket pods and other tactical stores including two Sidewinder AAMs
Powerplant: one 21,500-lb (9752-kg) thrust Rolls-Royce Pegasus 103

vectored-thrust turbofan
Performance: maximum speed at low level given as over 737 mph (1186 km/h); dive Mach limit 1.3; range with one inflight-refuelling over 3,455 miles (5560 km); endurance with one inflight-refuelling 7 hours
Weights: empty 11,959 lb (5425 kg); maximum take-off over 25,000 lb (11340 kg)
Dimensions: span 25 ft 3 in (7.7 m); length 46 ft 10 in (14.27 m); height 11 ft 4 in (3.45 m); wing area 201.0 sq ft (18.68 m²)

One of the free world's most important combat aircraft, the BAe Harrier serves only in limited numbers with the British and Americans. The example shown is an aircraft of No. 4 Squadron, RAF Germany, based at Gütersloh, which is the RAF's most easterly combat airfield. Notable are the revised nose with a laser ranger and marked target seeker, absence of the bolt-on inflight-refuelling probe and longer-span ferry wingtips, and external stores including two rocket pods and a pair of underfuselage 30-mm Aden cannon.

British and European Combat Aircraft

Progressive updating of the Harrier GR.Mk 3 force with laser noses and radar-warning passive receiver systems has subtly changed the profile and conferred a more purposeful look. This is a GR.Mk 3 serving with No. 3 Squadron.

The RAF's two-seaters are fully combat-capable and some have been retro-fitted with laser noses and radar-warning receivers. In any emergency they would become part of the RAF's small front-line forces. This Harrier T.Mk 4 is assigned to No. 4 Squadron.

BAe Harrier GR.Mk 3

1 Pitot tube
2 Laser protective 'eyelids'
3 Ferranti Laser Ranger and Marked Target Seeker unit (LRMTS)
4 Cooling air duct
5 Oblique camera
6 Camera port
7 Windshield washer reservoir
8 Inertial platform
9 Nose pitch reaction control air duct
10 Pitch feel and trim actuator
11 IFF aerial
12 Cockpit ram air intake
13 Yaw vane
14 Cockpit air discharge valve
15 Front pressure bulkhead
16 Rudder pedals
17 Nav/attack 'head-down' display unit
18 Underfloor control linkages
19 Canopy external handle
20 Control column
21 Instrument panel shroud
22 Windscreen wiper
23 Birdproof windscreen panels
24 Head-up display
25 Starboard side console panel
26 Nozzle angle control lever
27 Engine throttle lever
28 Ejection seat rocket pack
29 Fuel cock
30 Cockpit pressurization relief valve
31 Canopy emergency release
32 Pilot's Martin-Baker Type 9D zero-zero ejection seat
33 Sliding canopy rail
34 Miniature detonating cord (MDC) canopy breaker
35 Starboard air intake
36 Ejection seat headrest
37 Cockpit rear pressure bulkhead
38 Nose undercarriage wheel well
39 Boundary layer bleed air duct
40 Port air intake
41 Pre-closing nosewheel door
42 Landing/taxiing lamp
43 Nosewheel forks
44 Nosewheel

45 Supplementary air intake doors (fully floating)
46 Intake ducting
47 Hydraulic accumulator
48 Nosewheel retraction jack
49 Intake centre-body
50 Ram air discharge to engine intake
51 Cockpit air conditioning plant
52 Air conditioning system ram air intakes
53 Boundary layer bleed air discharge ducts
54 Starboard supplementary air intake doors
55 UHF aerial
56 Engine intake compressor face
57 Air refuelling probe connection
58 Forward fuselage integral fuel tank, port and starboard
59 Engine bay venting air scoop
60 Hydraulic ground connections
61 Engine monitoring and recording equipment
62 Forward nozzle fairing
63 Fan air (cold stream) swivelling nozzle
64 Nozzle bearing
65 Venting air intake
66 Alternator cooling air ducts
67 Twin alternators
68 Engine accessory gearbox
69 Alternator cooling air exhausts
70 Engine bay access doors
71 Gas turbine starter/ Auxiliary power unit, GTS/ APU

72 APU exhaust duct
73 Aileron control rods
74 Wing front spar carry-through
75 Nozzle bearing cooling air duct
76 Engine turbine section
77 Rolls-Royce Pegasus Mk 103 vectored thrust turbofan engine
78 Wing panel centreline joint rib

79 APU intake
80 Wing centre-section fairing panels
81 Starboard wing integral fuel tank, total internal fuel capacity 630 Imp gal (2865 litres)
82 Fuel system piping

© Pilot Press Limited

12

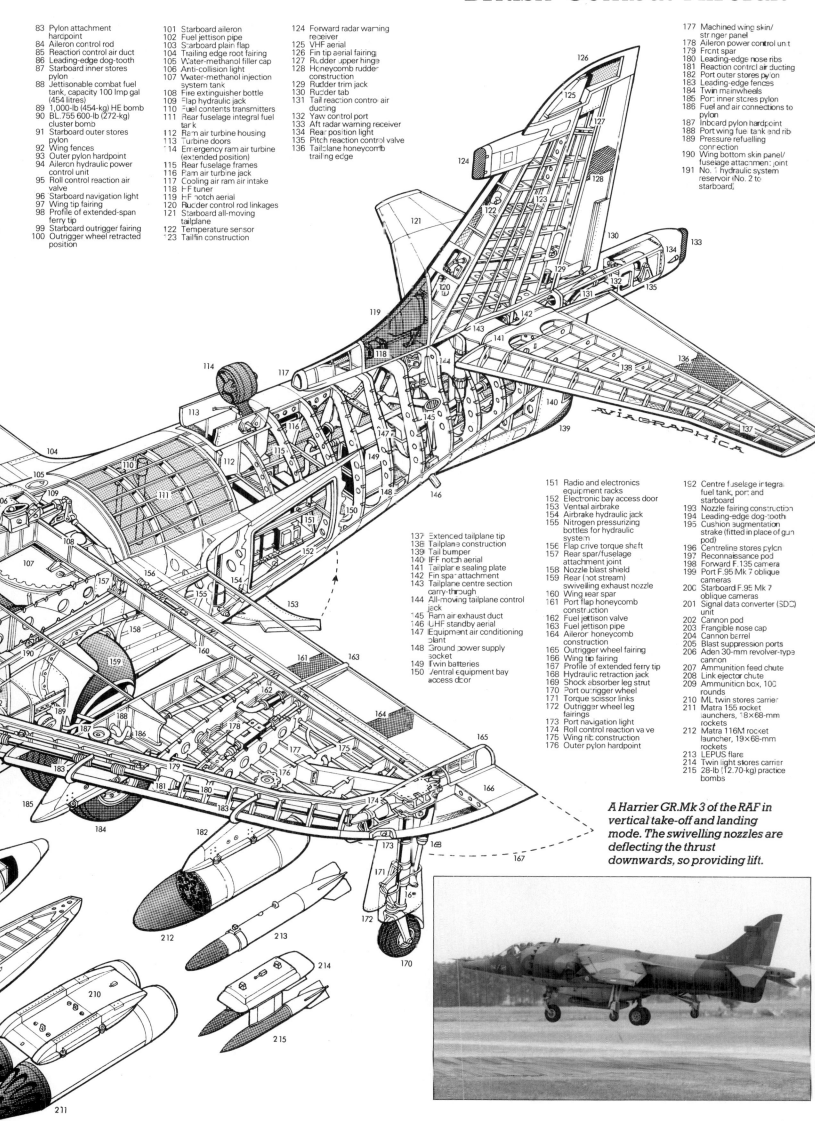

83 Pylon attachment hardpoint
84 Aileron control rod
85 Reaction control air duct
86 Leading-edge dog-tooth
87 Starboard inner stores pylon
88 Jettisonable combat fuel tank, capacity 100 Imp gal (454 litres)
89 1,000-lb (454-kg) HE bomb
90 BL.755 600-lb (272-kg) cluster bomb
91 Starboard outer stores pylon
92 Wing fences
93 Outer pylon hardpoint
94 Aileron hydraulic power control unit
95 Roll control reaction air valve
96 Starboard navigation light
97 Wing tip fairing
98 Profile of extended-span ferry tip
99 Starboard outrigger fairing
100 Outrigger wheel retracted position

101 Starboard aileron
102 Fuel jettison pipe
103 Starboard plain flap
104 Trailing edge root fairing
105 Water-methanol filler cap
106 Anti-collision light
107 Water-methanol injection system tank
108 Fire extinguisher bottle
109 Flap hydraulic jack
110 Fuel contents transmitters
111 Rear fuselage integral fuel tank
112 Ram air turbine housing
113 Turbine doors
114 Emergency ram air turbine (extended position)
115 Rear fuselage frames
116 Ram air turbine jack
117 Cooling air ram air intake
118 HF tuner
119 HF notch aerial
120 Rudder control rod linkages
121 Starboard all-moving tailplane
122 Temperature sensor
123 Tailfin construction

124 Forward radar warning receiver
125 VHF aerial
126 Fin tip aerial fairing
127 Rudder upper hinge
128 Honeycomb rudder construction
129 Rudder trim jack
130 Rudder tab
131 Tail reaction control air ducting
132 Yaw control port
133 Aft radar warning receiver
134 Rear position light
135 Pitch reaction control valve
136 Tailplane honeycomb trailing edge

137 Extended tailplane tip
138 Tailplane construction
139 Tail bumper
140 IFF notch aerial
141 Tailplane sealing plate
142 Fin spar attachment
143 Tailplane centre section carry-through
144 All-moving tailplane control jack
145 Ram air exhaust duct
146 UHF standby aerial
147 Equipment air conditioning plant
148 Ground power supply socket
149 Twin batteries
150 Ventral equipment bay access door

151 Radio and electronics equipment racks
152 Electronic bay access door
153 Ventral airbrake
154 Airbrake hydraulic jack
155 Nitrogen pressurizing bottles for hydraulic system
156 Flap drive torque shaft
157 Rear spar/fuselage attachment joint
158 Nozzle blast shield
159 Rear (hot stream) swivelling exhaust nozzle
160 Wing rear spar
161 Port flap honeycomb construction
162 Fuel jettison valve
163 Fuel jettison pipe
164 Aileron honeycomb construction
165 Outrigger wheel fairing
166 Wing tip fairing
167 Profile of extended ferry tip
168 Hydraulic retraction jack
169 Shock absorber leg strut
170 Port outrigger wheel
171 Torque scissor links
172 Outrigger wheel leg fairings
173 Port navigation light
174 Roll control reaction valve
175 Wing rib construction
176 Outer pylon hardpoint

177 Machined wing skin/stringer panel
178 Aileron power control unit
179 Front spar
180 Leading-edge nose ribs
181 Reaction control air ducting
182 Port outer stores pylon
183 Leading-edge fences
184 Twin mainwheels
185 Port inner stores pylon
186 Fuel and air connections to pylon
187 Inboard pylon hardpoint
188 Port wing fuel tank end rib
189 Pressure refuelling connection
190 Wing bottom skin panel/fuselage attachment joint
191 No. 1 hydraulic system reservoir (No. 2 to starboard)

192 Centre fuselage integral fuel tank, port and starboard
193 Nozzle fairing construction
194 Leading-edge dog-tooth
195 Cushion augmentation strake (fitted in place of gun pod)
196 Centreline stores pylon
197 Reconnaissance pod
198 Forward F.135 camera
199 Port F.95 Mk 7 oblique cameras
200 Starboard F.95 Mk 7 oblique cameras
201 Signal data converter (SDC) unit
202 Cannon pod
203 Frangible nose cap
204 Cannon barrel
205 Blast suppression ports
206 Aden 30-mm revolver-type cannon
207 Ammunition feed chute
208 Link ejector chute
209 Ammunition box, 100 rounds
210 ML twin stores carrier
211 Matra 155 rocket launchers, 18×68-mm rockets
212 Matra 116M rocket launcher, 19×68-mm rockets
213 LEPUS flare
214 Twin light stores carrier
215 28-lb (12.70-kg) practice bombs

A Harrier GR.Mk 3 of the RAF in vertical take-off and landing mode. The swivelling nozzles are deflecting the thrust downwards, so providing lift.

British Aerospace Sea Harrier

History and Notes
The versatility and effectiveness of a maritime version of the Harrier was evident by 1966, when the Harrier began flight development, but for political reasons little could be done until the go-ahead was given in May 1975. The first of an initial batch of 24 for the Royal Navy flew on 20 August 1978. Subsequently a further 10 were ordered, followed by 14 in July 1982 (seven of the latter replacing attrition in RN service, including the Falklands war). Another six, Sea Harrier Mk 51s, have been ordered by the Indian navy. All are basically similar, with a new forward fuselage seating the pilot higher to provide space for extra avionics and extra panel space for cockpit controls. The nose houses a double-folding Ferranti Blue Fox multi-mode radar, and the raised canopy gives the pilot a good all-round view. Nav/attack systems include a twin-gyro platform and Doppler, giving inertial accuracy without the warm-up or ship-based problems and at lower cost. An extremely wide spectrum of weapons, sensors and missions can be handled, the basic RN machine having the designation FRS for fighter/reconnaissance/strike. The suggestion that Sea Harriers could not fly fighter missions was soon dispelled by the 20-0 score gained in the South Atlantic in air combat. Sea Harriers pioneered the 12° ski jump used in RN and Spanish V/STOL carriers.

Specification: British Aerospace Sea Harrier FRS.Mk 1
Origin: UK
Type: V/STOL ship-based multi-role combat aircraft
Armament: two 30-mm Aden cannon each with 125 rounds (optional); underwing loads can include all weapons of Harrier plus AIM-9L or (India) Magic AAMs and Sea Eagle, Harpoon or other anti-ship missiles
Powerplant: one 21,500-lb (9752-kg) thrust Rolls-Royce Pegasus 104

The Sea Harrier FRS.Mk 1 of the Royal Navy uses an airframe almost identical with the RAF GR.Mk 3 except for the new forward fuselage with raised cockpit, extra avionics and folding radar. This FRS.Mk 1 serves with No. 800 Squadron on HMS Invincible.

vectored-thrust turbofan
Performance: maximum speed 'over 736 mph (1185 km/h)'; dive limit Mach 1.25; radius without inflight-refuelling (high-altitude interception) 460 miles (750 km), or (low-level strike) 288 miles (463 km)
Weights: not published in late 1982 but similar to those of the Harrier, and maximum weapon load given as 8,000 lb (3629 kg)
Dimensions: span 25 ft 3 in (7.7 m); length 47 ft 7 in (14.5 m); height 12 ft 2 in (3.71 m); wing area 201.1 sq ft (18.68 m²)

BAe Sea Harrier FRS.Mk 1

BAe Sea Harrier with early low-visibility paint scheme.

Aircraft of No. 809 Squadron which arrived in the Falklands in May 1982 were painted in medium sea grey, with Barley grey on the wing and tailplane undersurfaces. This aircraft, XZ499, shot down one Argentine Dassault-Breguet Mirage III during the Falklands war.

During the final stages of the Falklands operation two Sea Harriers landed aboard ships other than the carriers HMS Hermes and Invincible; a Sidewinder-armed Sea Harrier is seen here landing on the amphibious assault cruiser HMS Intrepid.

The Sea Harrier's maximum take-off weight can be increased with the use of a ramp or 'ski-jump', as demonstrated by an aircraft of the training unit, No. 899 Squadron. Note the close proximity of Sea King ASW helicopters to the ramp – a clear indication of the space restrictions aboard aircraft carriers.

British and European Combat Aircraft

Royal Navy Sea Harriers from (top to bottom) Nos 800, 899 and 801 Squadrons. It was not to be long before this very capable aircraft found itself in action; in the early summer of 1982 both Nos 800 and 801 Squadrons were deployed against Argentine aircraft, ships and ground targets during the Falklands conflict.

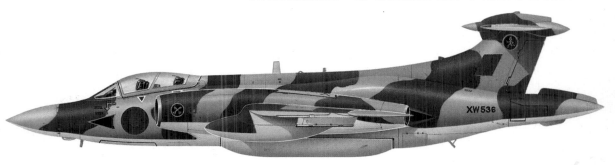

Twenty-five years after the type's first flight, the Blackburn Buccaneer is still in service with the RAF. This aircraft is a Spey-powered Buccaneer S.Mk 2B which served at RAF Laarbruch, Germany with No. 16 Squadron in the nuclear strike role during the late 1970s. Several aircraft were retired after severe metal fatigue was found following a Buccaneer crash in America.

two-seaters), which it christened the Matador. Well pleased with the AV-8A's performance in the close-support role, the US Marines announced a programme to add aerodynamic lift-improvement devices to existing Harriers, changing their designation to AV-8C, and McDonnell Douglas in the USA has been commissioned to produce a considerably modified and improved version as the AV-8B Harrier II. The first of an eventual 412 AV-8Bs flew on 5 November 1981, the order including 60 to be assembled in the UK as Harrier GR.Mk 5s for the RAF, and a dozen for Spain.

Navalized V/STOL air power

Although a prototype P.1127 landed on the aircraft carrier HMS *Ark Royal* in February 1963, it was not until May 1975 that the fully-navalized P.1184 Sea Harrier FRS.Mk 1 was ordered into production for the Fleet Air Arm (FAA) to serve aboard three new 'through-deck' cruisers of the 'Invincible' class. Charged with interception as well as strike duties, the Sea Harrier is equipped with nose-mounted Blue Fox radar in place of the laser rangefinder of its land-based counterpart, and is armed with Sidewinder AAMs as well as the recently-developed Sea Eagle anti-ship missile.

Flown for the first time on 20 August 1978, the aircraft made its initial deck landing three months later, and joined an operational seagoing squadron (No. 800) in March 1980. Its combat debut occurred on 1 May 1982 when Sea Harriers from HMS *Invincible* and the aircraft-carrier HMS *Hermes* (both fitted with a deck ramp or 'ski-jump' for enhanced aircraft take-off performance with full weapons load) bombed airfields occupied by Argentine forces after their invasion of the Falkland Islands. In seven weeks of intensive strike and air defence operations which followed, 28 Sea Harriers destroyed 20 opposing aircraft for the loss of only two of their number to ground fire. Eight Sea Harriers have been delivered to the Indian Navy in addition to 48 on order for the FAA.

An earlier generation of naval aircraft, now exclusively with the RAF since HMS *Ark Royal* was retired in December 1978, is represented by the Blackburn (later Hawker Siddeley) Buccaneer. Produced to specification NA.39, the Buccaneer was the world's first strike aircraft designed specifically for low-level missions below the coverage of enemy radar, its strangely-shaped rear

Threading their way through the Scottish Highlands at low level, two Buccaneer S.Mk 2Bs of No. 208 Squadron undertake a training sortie with practice bombs mounted in carriers on the outer wing pylons. The RAF will retain Buccaneers in the maritime strike role until the early 1990s.

In later service with RAF Germany, Lightnings were painted matt dark green on upper surfaces to suit their operations. This F.Mk 2A of No. 92 Squadron is shown as it appeared at Gütersloh in 1975 with Firestreak missiles. The unit badge is composed of a cobra and maple sprig.

fuselage also testifying to its status as the first British aircraft to employ aerodynamic 'area rule' for enhanced performance.

Twenty trials aircraft were flown from 30 April 1958 onwards, and after 40 Gyron Junior-engined Buccaneer S.Mk 1s, production turned to the Spey-powered Buccaneer S.Mk 2, of which 133 were built up to September 1977, including 46 to RAF orders. Five RAF squadrons were assigned Buccaneers, beginning with No. 12 which formed in October 1969 with aircraft transferred from the Royal Navy, the definitive Buccaneer S.Mk 2B having provision for Martel ASMs in addition to bombs mounted in the rotating underfuselage weapons bay. Two Buccaneer squadrons in RAF Germany will shortly have their aircraft replaced by Panavia Tornadoes, but a further two are to remain in the anti-shipping role (soon with Sea Eagle ASMs) until the early 1990s. Six survivors of 16 Buccaneer S.Mk 50s still serve the South African Air Force.

Long service Lightning

Like the Buccaneer, the English Electric Lightning is another 1950s' vintage aircraft remaining in the RAF's front line and still highly popular with its pilots, despite its ageing avionics. Derived from the P.1 high-speed research aircraft which made its initial flight in 4 August 1954, the Lightning entered service with No. 74 Squadron at Coltishall in June 1960 to become the RAF's first supersonic interceptor. Twenty-five prototype and trials P.1s were built, followed by 216 single-seat Lightning F.Mks 1, 1A, 2, 2A, 3, 3A and 6, plus 44 Lightning T.Mk 4 and T.Mk 5 trainers, these forming the backbone of what was then Fighter Command. Export orders accounted for 40 to Saudi Arabia and 14 to Kuwait, excluding transfers from the RAF, before production ended in 1969.

In the heyday of its career, the Lightning served with units in Germany, Cyprus and Singapore in addition to home-based squadrons, but now Kuwait's aircraft have been retired and Saudi Arabian Lightnings are to do so in the early 1980s, leaving just over 60 Lightning F.Mk 3s, F.Mk 6s and T.Mk 5s in British service with two squadrons until replaced by Tornado F.Mk 2s in 1986-7.

During 1982, RAF Lightnings began to exchange their green and grey camouflage for two-tone light grey colours, following the lead set by air defence Phantoms. This Lightning F.Mk 6, flown by the commanding officer of No. 5 Squadron at Binbrook, is armed with two Red Top missiles and a pair of 30-mm Aden cannon mounted in the belly tank.

Some African countries demand confidentiality in their arms purchases, and this was certainly true in the case of Kenya, although the 12 BAe Hawk Mk 52s contracted in 1978 and delivered in 1980 have featured in local newspapers. Nonetheless, BAe still refers to these aircraft as being for 'an unnamed African country'.

The latest (and possibly the last) of the 50-series export Hawks with Adour 851 engines, the Indonesian air force Mk 53 has been the subject of a series of small contracts, which currently cover 17 aircraft (the first of which is illustrated here). Like other export Hawks, the Mk 53 is equally suited to training and ground attack.

The sale of Hawks to Finland (illustrated here by the first Mk 51) represented a major breakthrough for BAe, in view of the number of aircraft involved (50) and the fact that the sale was won in the face of intense competition from Dassault-Breguet and Saab-Scania. Some 46 are to be assembled by Valmet in Finland.

The BAe Hawk can double up as a light support aircraft, and here a Hawk T.Mk 1 of No. 1 Tactical Weapons Unit, based at RAF Brawdy and wearing the markings of No. 234 Squadron (one of No. 1 TWU's 'shadow' squadrons) discharges an impressive ripple salvo of folding-fin rockets over a weapons range.

British Aerospace Hawk

History and Notes
Originally the Hawker Siddeley P.1182, this trainer was the first British military aircraft for more than a decade. Its development was swift, and so successful that the type handsomely exceeded specification in almost every parameter. Powered by an economical and long-lived turbofan engine, the Hawk has an airframe of strength and fatigue life never before equalled in a small jet, and in systems design it was judged 'in a class of its own' by the US Navy during a long and detailed evaluation in 1980-1. No prototype was built, the first five off the line being allocated to flight trials, begun on 21 August 1974. Deliveries began in 1976 and by late 1982 RAF Hawks had flown 165,000 hours with a safety record unmatched by any known military type (one aircraft has been lost, after colliding with a ship's mast). A number (possibly 90) will serve as second-line interceptors with AIM-9L missiles whilst continuing as weapon trainers at Brawdy. In November 1981 the US Navy selected the Hawk as its new-generation trainer, assembled by McDonnell Douglas at Long Beach and procured initially as the T-45B for airfield use (with new carrier-type landing gear, twin speed brakes and new cockpit) for use from 1988, and as the T-45A (with new nose, rear fuselage and hook) for carrier use from 1991. Other Hawks include the Mk 51 (Finland), Mk 52 (Kenya), Mk 53 (Indonesia) and Mk 60 (Zimbabwe, with 5,700-lb/2586-kg thrust Mk 861 engines). Export Hawks can have five pylons for a 6,800-lb (3085-kg) weapon load and advanced F-16 type nav/attack avionics.

Specification: British Aerospace Hawk T.Mk 1
Origin: UK
Type: multirole trainer and attack/defence
Armament: centreline 30-mm Aden cannon pod (optional) plus up to 1,500 lb (680 kg) of practice stores; capability for a 5,660-lb (2567-kg) weapon load

This RAF Hawk T.Mk 1 is shown in the high visibility red and white paint scheme of No. 4 Flying Training School at RAF Valley in North Wales.

including AIM-9L or other AAMs, and export aircraft can carry 6,800 lb (3085 kg) of ordnance
Powerplant: one 5,200-lb (2359-kg) thrust Rolls-Royce/Turboméca Adour 151 turbofan
Performance: maximum speed 645 mph (1038 km/h); dive limit Mach 1.2; combat radius 345 miles (556 km) with 5,660-lb (2567-kg) weapon load, or 645 miles (1038 km) with 3,000-lb (1361-kg) load
Weights: empty 8,040 lb (3647 kg); maximum take-off 17,085 lb (7750 kg)
Dimensions: span 30 ft 9¾ in (9.39 m); length, excluding probe 36 ft 7¾ in (11.17 m); height 13 ft 1¼ in (3.99 m); wing area 179.6 sq ft (16.69 m²)

BAe Hawk T.Mk 1 (lower side view: proposed attack version)

BAe Hawk Mk 53, prior to delivery to Indonesia.

The Red Arrows as they go over the top of a formation loop, trailing smoke. Due to its outstanding handling characteristics and good thrust/weight ratio, the Hawk is a highly suitable aircraft for team aerobatics, and its very low fuel consumption makes it economical to operate. In war, these aircraft would be used in air defence.

British Combat Aircraft

In view of the United States' capability to produce its own military aircraft, the supreme accolade for any European manufacturer must be to have its product ordered for the US forces. Having supplied the Harrier to the Marines, BAe's Kingston-Brough Division has recently followed with a second coup in gaining acceptance for the Hawk advanced trainer from the US Navy. Produced as a successor to the Folland Gnat T.Mk 1 and originally known as the Hawker Siddeley P.1182, the Hawk was ordered 'off the drawing board' for the RAF to the extent of 176 aircraft, the prototype flying on 21 August 1974.

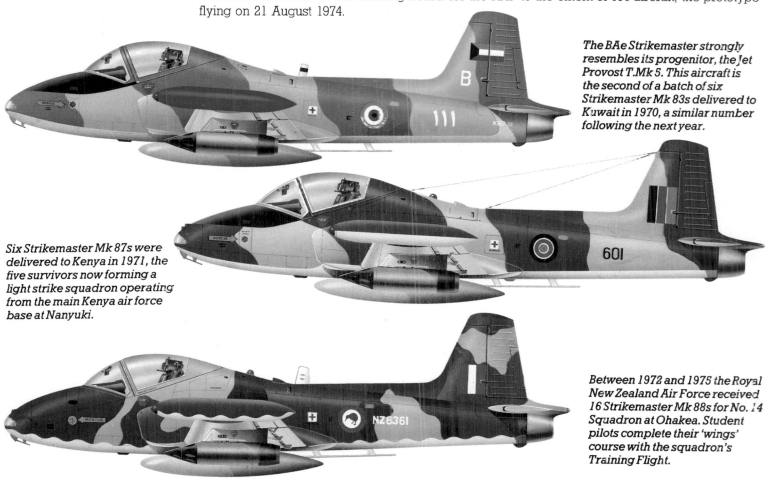

The BAe Strikemaster strongly resembles its progenitor, the Jet Provost T.Mk 5. This aircraft is the second of a batch of six Strikemaster Mk 83s delivered to Kuwait in 1970, a similar number following the next year.

Six Strikemaster Mk 87s were delivered to Kenya in 1971, the five survivors now forming a light strike squadron operating from the main Kenya air force base at Nanyuki.

Between 1972 and 1975 the Royal New Zealand Air Force received 16 Strikemaster Mk 88s for No. 14 Squadron at Ohakea. Student pilots complete their 'wings' course with the squadron's Training Flight.

BAe Strikemasters are used for training by the Royal Saudi air force. Aircraft of No. 11 Squadron, pictured overflying typical desert terrain, are assigned to weapons instruction.

British and European Combat Aircraft

Entering service in November 1976 with the Central Flying School, the Hawk T.Mk 1 is used by the RAF for both pure flying instruction and weapons training, its high level of reliability and excellent handling qualities making it a natural choice for the internationally-famous Red Arrows aerobatic team, to which it was issued in time for the 1980 air display season. Subsequently, 90 Hawks of the Red Arrows and the tactical weapons training units have been modified to carry Sidewinder AAMs for air defence duties in an emergency.

Foreign interest in the aircraft's light-attack capabilities has resulted in orders from Kenya (12 aircraft), Finland (50), Indonesia (17), Zimbabwe (eight) and UAE (eight), and in 1981 the Hawk was chosen as the US Navy's next-generation pilot-training aircraft, with the military designation T-45. The US Navy requires 254 fully-navalized T-45As to be operational as aircraft-carrier trainers from the early-1990s onwards and 54 land-based T-45Bs on line in 1988, all to be built under licence in the USA by McDonnell Douglas. A new version, the Hawk 100, has been proposed by BAe exclusively for the strike role, with additional avionics to assist navigation and target-acquisition.

Ocean hunter

No review of the RAF's front-line equipment would be complete without mention of the Nimrod, a long-range maritime reconnaissance aircraft unique in its employment of four jet engines, rather than the turboprops of equivalents such as the Lockheed Orion. Based on the Comet airliner, the Hawker Siddeley 801 Nimrod MR.Mk 1 flew on 23 May 1967 and joined the RAF two years later, two prototypes being followed by 46 production aircraft and three electronic intelligence-gathering Nimrod R.Mk 1s.

Tasked with tracking submarines and surface vessels on long sorties over the Atlantic while cruising on two engines when on its 'beat', the Nimrod has had its detection capabilities improved substantially with retrospective installation of Searchwater radar, Barra sonobuoys and associated AQS-901 data-processing equipment in the Nimrod MR.Mk 2 version. Eleven aircraft are in the process of conversion to Nimrod AEW.Mk 3 standard through fitment of Marconi Mission System Avionics in two bulbous radomes at the nose and tail. First flown on 16 July 1980, the Nimrod AEW.Mk 3 will patrol far from base to provide much enhanced airborne early warning and control systems (AWACS) for detection of low-level attacks against the United Kingdom and direction of defensive interceptors, as a parallel to NATO's fleet of Boeing E-3A Sentries.

The Pilatus/Britten-Norman Islander, a popular aircraft with civilian operators, has also been adopted for light transport duties with several air forces. With provision for light armament beneath the wings – as illustrated here in the markings of the Omani air force – it is known as the Defender.

The aptly-named Shorts Skyvan is a rugged light transport design for both civilian and military operations from short and semi-prepared airstrips. One of dozen air forces to operate the type is that of Oman, which received 16 for use by its No. 2 Squadron, based at Seeb.

*Eleven Nimrod AEW.Mk 3s –
converted from MR.Mk 1
airframes – are entering RAF
service in the airborne early
warning role as counterparts to
the USAF and NATO Boeing E-3A
Sentries. The aircraft wear a coat
of hemp camouflage on their
upper surfaces and are
expected to be equipped with
flight-refuelling probes above
the cockpit.*

*Nimrod MR.Mk 2 in the hemp
and light grey finish adopted in
1980. The RAF's force of Nimrods
is used by No. 18 Maritime Group.*

*Protection of maritime resources
is today as important a role as
the more traditional one of anti-
submarine warfare and fleet
protection. Here a Royal Air
Force Nimrod MR.Mk 1 patrols
over a North Sea oil rig.*

French Military Aircraft

Second only to the USSR and USA as an exporter of armaments, France has built up a competitive aircraft industry led by the versatile Mirage family of fighters and supported by a home market ever ready to purchase the latest technology.

Among several types of Mirage operated by the South African Air Force, the Mirage F.1AZ is used by No. 1 Squadron in the strike role with a range of armament including rocket pods.

The Mirage IIICZ provides the South African Air Force with a potent force of fighter bombers for ground attack duties along its borders. This aircraft flies with No. 2 Squadron based at Hoedspruit.

The remarkable renaissance of the French aircraft industry following its obliteration during World War II is nowhere more graphically apparent than in the worldwide sales success enjoyed by the Dassault-Breguet Mirage III, Mirage 5 and Mirage 50 family. After producing useful but unspectacular aircraft during the 1950s, Avions Marcel Dassault (as it then was) flew the delta-winged Mirage I prototype for the first time on 25 June 1955, the Mirage III following on 17 November 1956. The potential of the aircraft as an interceptor and fighter-bomber was quickly appreciated both at home and abroad, and a trials batch of 10 Mirage IIIAs was followed by large-scale production for the French air force.

Mirage IIICs began their operational service as interceptors with the 2e Escadre de Chasse (2nd Fighter Wing) of l'Armée de l'Air in July 1961, and 95 were produced to local order before the 13e Escadre de Chasse accepted the first of an eventual 183 Mirage IIIEs optimized for the tactical strike role in July 1965. With its radar nose replaced by camera bays, the Mirage IIIE became the

British and European Combat Aircraft

Mirage 5COA (3029) of Grupo de Combate 1, Fuerza Aérea Colombiana, at German Olano AB, Palanquero. In 1970 Colombia purchased a force of 14 Mirage 5COA fighter bombers, two COR reconnaissance aircraft and two COD two-seat trainers.

This Mirage 5PA wears the markings of the Pakistani air force and probably serves with No. 9 Operational Conversion Unit at Rafiqui.

Mirage 5BA of the 2e Wing's 2e Escadrille de Chasseurs-Bombardiers of the Force Aérienne Belge, this unit being based at Florennes with the Mirage 5BRs of the 42e, the wing's tactical reconnaissance unit.

Mirage IIIR tactical reconnaissance variant, 70 of which were absorbed by 33e Escadre de Reconnaissance from March 1963 onwards. Training was provided by the two-seat Mirage IIIB, French orders for 63 including 20 Mirage IIIBEs with systems similar to the Mirage IIIE.

A dozen export orders were received for the Mirage III, of which 112 were acquired by Australia and mostly built locally by the Commonwealth Aircraft Corporation. Combat experience was gained by Israeli Mirage IIICJs in several skirmishes with neighbouring Arab air forces and full-scale wars during 1967 and 1973, the first combat success by the aircraft being gained against a Syrian MiG-17 on 20 August 1963. Pakistani aircraft were in action against India in December 1971, whilst more recently Argentine Mirages fought British Sea Harriers over the Falkland Islands in May and June 1982.

Fresh from overhaul, a Pakistani air force Dassault-Breguet Mirage IIIEP (right) awaits resupply to No. 5 Squadron. The Mirage has seen much service with Pakistan, fighting in its wars with India in 1971, and it is likely to serve for at least a further decade.

Simplified for export

Further customers were attracted to the Mirage following the first flight on 19 May 1967 of a simplified and cheaper variant lacking radar, known as the Mirage 5. An early production order for 50 placed by Israel was embargoed, the aircraft going instead to the French air force, which bestowed the designation Mirage 5F, whilst Belgium built 103 of its 106 Mirage 5BA strike aircraft, Mirage 5BR reconnaissance models and Mirage 5BD trainers under licence. Many others went to Arab and Latin American air arms, and Israel 'obtained' the necessary technical drawings to produce its own version as the Nesher, later adding an American J79 engine in the definitive Kfir.

Dassault also substituted the higher-powered Atar 09K-50 engine for the earlier Atar 09C to give

Operational conversion to Switzerland's Mirage IIIS interceptors is undertaken on the tandem-seat trainer version, the IIIBS. Mirages having a B or D suffix are trainers, the second letter in this case indicating the customer country. Mirage IIIS and IIIBS aircraft are operated from Emmen by Fliegerstaffeln 16 and 17, whilst FlSt 10 flies 18 reconnaissance-configured IIIRS variants from Dübendorf.

PAINT SHOP

British and European Combat Aircraft

History and Notes
One of the most famous fighters in history, the basic Mirage Delta stemmed from Dassault's disbelief in the French official light-fighter concept, and his decision at company expense to build a larger tailless delta Mirage powered by an Atar engine. The Mirage III-001 flew on 17 November 1956 and the first production Mirage IIIC for l'Armée de l'Air flew in 1960, to be followed by more than 1,400 basically similar machines for 21 countries. Early models could have a booster rocket engine under the rear in place of gun ammunition and a fuel tank. The large main wheels were sized for rough-field operation, though this is nullified by the very high take-off and landing speeds giving field lengths over 6,000 ft (1.8 km) on attack missions. The Mirage IIIB and IIID were tandem dual versions, the Mirage IIIE series are fighter-bombers with extra weapon-delivery systems (French Mirage IIIEs carry the AG52 nuclear bomb) and Mirage IIIR reconnaissance aircraft have a distinctive camera nose replacing the Cyrano II radar. South African Mirage III CZ, DZ and RZ Mirages have the 15,873-lb (7200-kg) thrust Atar 9K50 engine which is standard in the Mirage 50 first flown in 1979 and with upgraded avionics (so far bought by Chile). In contrast the popular Mirage 5 is a clear-weather day attack aircraft with extra fuel and weapons replacing the radar and other avionics (various radar and laser/HUD options are available).

Specification: Dassault-Breguet Mirage IIIE
Origin: France
Type: fighter/bomber
Armament: two 30-mm cannon each with 125 rounds (no rocket); three external pylons for 1,000-lb (454-kg) bombs or equivalent stores including pods, tanks, AS.30 missiles or, for air/air role, an R.530 or Super 530 AAM plus two Sidewinder or Magic AAMs
Powerplant: one 13,670-lb (6200-kg) thrust SNECMA Atar 9C afterburning turbojet
Performance: maximum speed, clean at 39,370 ft (12000 m), 1,460 mph (2350 km/h), or clean at sea level 863 mph (1390 km/h); radius on a hi-lo-hi attack mission with one bomb and two tanks 745 miles (1200 km)
Weights: empty 15,540 lb (7050 kg); maximum take-off 30,200 lb (13700 kg)
Dimensions: span 26 ft 11½ in (8.22 m); length 49 ft 3½ in (15.03 m); height 14 ft 9in (4.5 m); wing area 374.6 sq ft (34.85 m²)

Dassault-Breguet Mirage III

A Mirage IIIC of the Israeli air force (Heyl Ha'Avir), equipped with two Shafrir short-range air-to-air missiles and supersonic external tanks. The roundels on the nose indicate that this aircraft has shot down 11 Egyptian opponents. Israel has received 72 Mirage IIICJs and five BJs, which have now been withdrawn.

Dassault-Breguet Mirage III

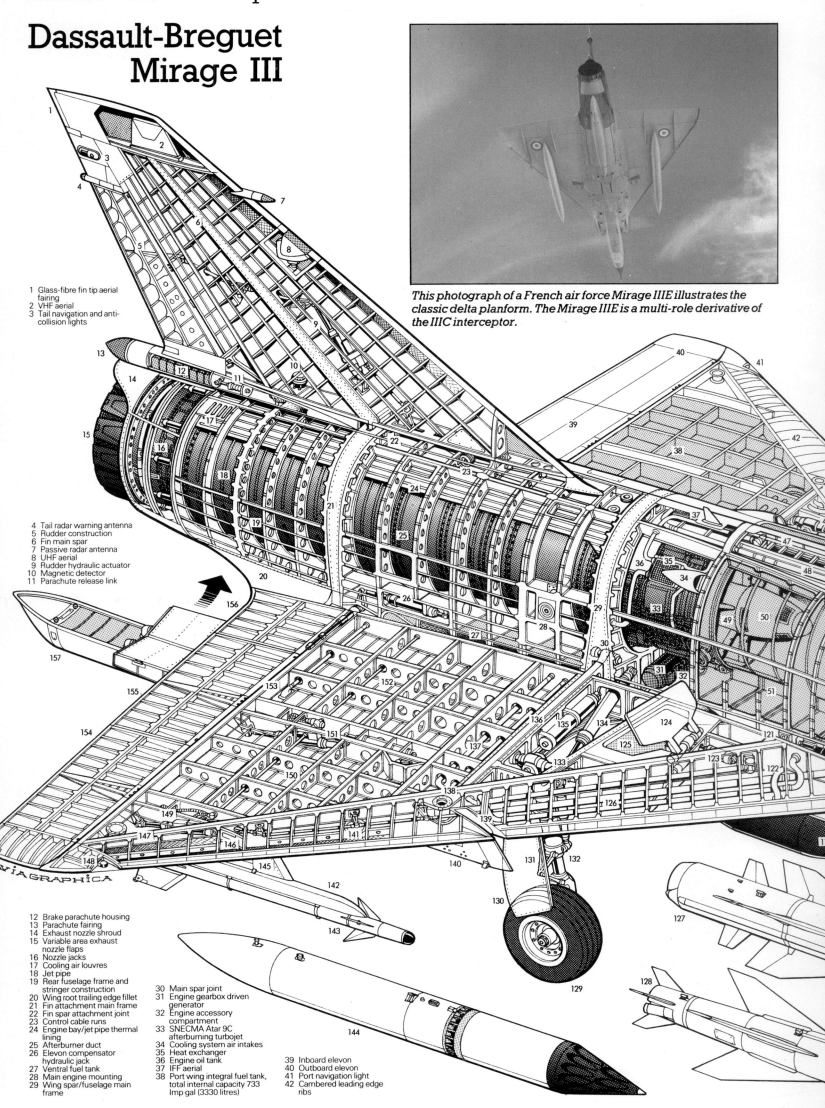

This photograph of a French air force Mirage IIIE illustrates the classic delta planform. The Mirage IIIE is a multi-role derivative of the IIIC interceptor.

1 Glass-fibre fin tip aerial fairing
2 VHF aerial
3 Tail navigation and anti-collision lights

4 Tail radar warning antenna
5 Rudder construction
6 Fin main spar
7 Passive radar antenna
8 UHF aerial
9 Rudder hydraulic actuator
10 Magnetic detector
11 Parachute release link

12 Brake parachute housing
13 Parachute fairing
14 Exhaust nozzle shroud
15 Variable area exhaust nozzle flaps
16 Nozzle jacks
17 Cooling air louvres
18 Jet pipe
19 Rear fuselage frame and stringer construction
20 Wing root trailing edge fillet
21 Fin attachment main frame
22 Fin spar attachment joint
23 Control cable runs
24 Engine bay/jet pipe thermal lining
25 Afterburner duct
26 Elevon compensator hydraulic jack
27 Ventral fuel tank
28 Main engine mounting
29 Wing spar/fuselage main frame

30 Main spar joint
31 Engine gearbox driven generator
32 Engine accessory compartment
33 SNECMA Atar 9C afterburning turbojet
34 Cooling system air intakes
35 Heat exchanger
36 Engine oil tank
37 IFF aerial
38 Port wing integral fuel tank, total internal capacity 733 Imp gal (3330 litres)

39 Inboard elevon
40 Outboard elevon
41 Port navigation light
42 Cambered leading edge ribs

AViAGRAPHiCA

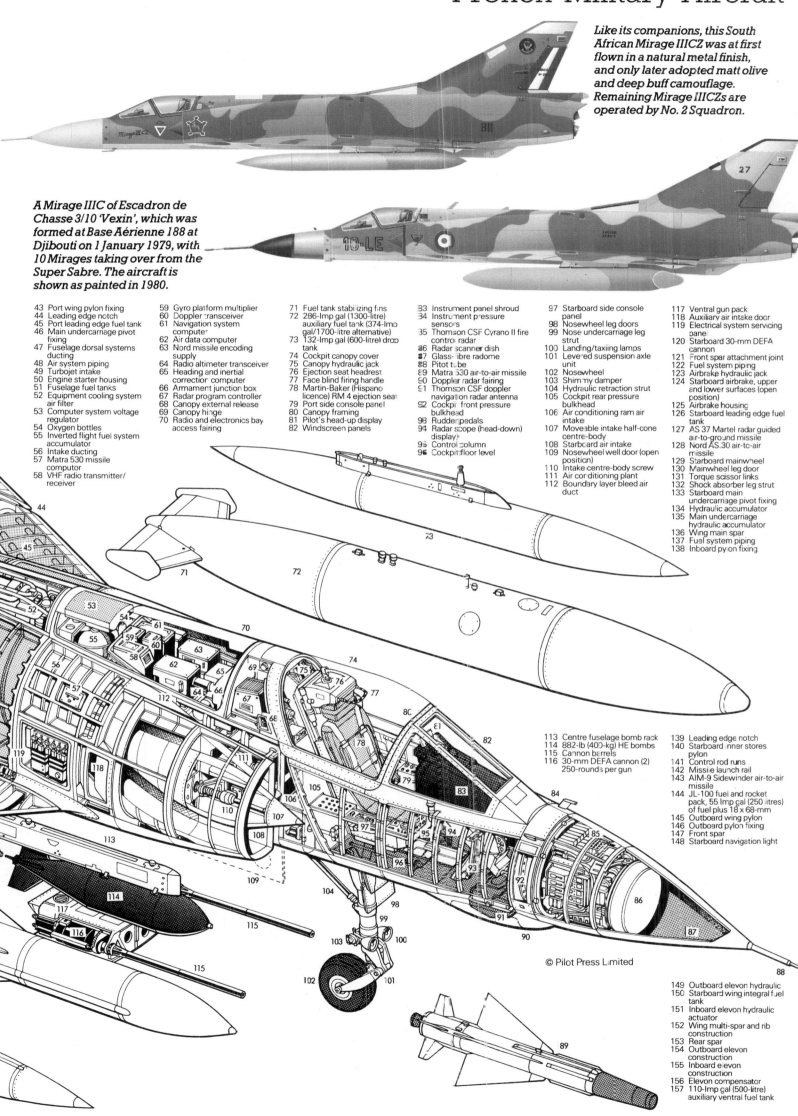

Like its companions, this South African Mirage IIICZ was at first flown in a natural metal finish, and only later adopted matt olive and deep buff camouflage. Remaining Mirage IIICZs are operated by No. 2 Squadron.

A Mirage IIIC of Escadron de Chasse 3/10 'Vexin', which was formed at Base Aérienne 188 at Djibouti on 1 January 1979, with 10 Mirages taking over from the Super Sabre. The aircraft is shown as painted in 1980.

43 Port wing pylon fixing
44 Leading edge notch
45 Port leading edge fuel tank
46 Main undercarriage pivot fixing
47 Fuselage dorsal systems ducting
48 Air system piping
49 Turbojet intake
50 Engine starter housing
51 Fuselage fuel tanks
52 Equipment cooling system air filter
53 Computer system voltage regulator
54 Oxygen bottles
55 Inverted flight fuel system accumulator
56 Intake ducting
57 Matra 530 missile computor
58 VHF radio transmitter/receiver

59 Gyro platform multiplier
60 Doppler transceiver
61 Navigation system computer
62 Air data computer
63 Nord missile encoding supply
64 Radio altimeter transceiver
65 Heading and inertial corrector computer
66 Armament junction box
67 Radar program controller
68 Canopy external release
69 Canopy hinge
70 Radio and electronics bay access fairing

71 Fuel tank stabilizing fins
72 286-Imp gal (1300-litre) auxiliary fuel tank (374-Imp gal/1700-litre alternative)
73 132-Imp gal (600-litre) drop tank
74 Cockpit canopy cover
75 Canopy hydraulic jack
76 Ejection seat headrest
77 Face blind firing handle
78 Martin-Baker (Hispano licence) RM 4 ejection seat
79 Port side console panel
80 Canopy framing
81 Pilot's head-up display
82 Windscreen panels

83 Instrument panel shroud
84 Instrument pressure sensors
85 Thomson CSF Cyrano II fire control radar
86 Radar scanner dish
87 Glass-fibre radome
88 Pitot tube
89 Matra 530 air-to-air missile
90 Doppler radar fairing
91 Thomson CSF doppler navigation radar antenna
92 Cockpit front pressure bulkhead
93 Rudder pedals
94 Radar scope (head-down) display
95 Control column
96 Cockpit floor level

97 Starboard side console panel
98 Nosewheel leg doors
99 Nose undercarriage leg strut
100 Landing/taxiing lamps
101 Levered suspension axle unit
102 Nosewheel
103 Shimmy damper
104 Hydraulic retraction strut
105 Cockpit rear pressure bulkhead
106 Air conditioning ram air intake
107 Moveable intake half-cone centre-body
108 Starboard air intake
109 Nosewheel well door (open position)
110 Intake centre-body screw
111 Air conditioning plant
112 Boundary layer bleed air duct

117 Ventral gun pack
118 Auxiliary air intake door
119 Electrical system servicing panel
120 Starboard 30-mm DEFA cannon
121 Front spar attachment joint
122 Fuel system piping
123 Airbrake hydraulic jack
124 Starboard airbrake, upper and lower surfaces (open position)
125 Airbrake housing
126 Starboard leading edge fuel tank
127 AS 37 Martel radar guided air-to-ground missile
128 Nord AS.30 air-to-air missile
129 Starboard mainwheel
130 Mainwheel leg door
131 Torque scissor links
132 Shock absorber leg strut
133 Starboard main undercarriage pivot fixing
134 Hydraulic accumulator
135 Main undercarriage hydraulic accumulator
136 Wing main spar
137 Fuel system piping
138 Inboard pylon fixing

113 Centre fuselage bomb rack
114 882-lb (400-kg) HE bombs
115 Cannon barrels
116 30-mm DEFA cannon (2) 250-rounds per gun

139 Leading edge notch
140 Starboard inner stores pylon
141 Control rod runs
142 Missile launch rail
143 AIM-9 Sidewinder air-to-air missile
144 JL-100 fuel and rocket pack, 55 Imp gal (250 litres) of fuel plus 18 x 68-mm
145 Outboard wing pylon
146 Outboard pylon fixing
147 Front spar
148 Starboard navigation light

© Pilot Press Limited

149 Outboard elevon hydraulic
150 Starboard wing integral fuel tank
151 Inboard elevon hydraulic actuator
152 Wing multi-spar and rib construction
153 Rear spar
154 Outboard elevon construction
155 Inboard elevon construction
156 Elevon compensator
157 110-Imp gal (500-litre) auxiliary ventral fuel tank

British and European Combat Aircraft

Mirage F.1CE of Escuadron 141 of Ala de Caza 14, one of three wings that make up the Mando de Combate of the Spanish air force (Ejercito del Aire).

Mirage F.1CZ of No. 3 Squadron, South African Air Force, based at Waterkloof. The SAAF uses a mixture of F.1AZs and F.1CZs in the strike and interception roles respectively.

the appropriately-numbered Mirage 50, although when first examples were supplied to South Africa in 1974 for reconnaissance duties they were known as Mirage IIIR-2Zs, and it was not until 15 April 1979 that the first true Mirage 50 was flown, production deliveries beginning to Chile in September 1980.

The Mirage III, Mirage 5 and Mirage 50 remain in small-scale production, with almost 1,400 now completed, but such is the basic soundness of the design that new variants are even now being proposed by Dassault. For close tailoring to customer's requirements, the Mirage 50 series is currently available in two forms: the confusingly-labelled III/50 with Cyrano IV radar for interception, and the strike-optimized Mirage 5/50 with Agave radar. But the most recent development, flown on 21 December 1982, is the Mirage IIING. This latest of the line has the new fly-by-wire control system and forward-fuselage canards for enhanced combat handling, a re-vamping of the basic design which may well result in the trusty Mirage rolling off the assembly track for many more years to come.

New export triumph

When Dassault received a French government contract to design a successor to the Mirage III early in 1964, the company elected to retain the name Mirage even though the new product was very different in design to its predecessor. In fact, whilst producing the two-seat Mirage F.2 to the official specification, Dassault also built a private-venture single-seater, flown for the first time on 23 December 1966, and it was this which gained the production order as the Mirage F.1. Forsaking the delta wing for a more conventional configuration, the Mirage F.1 has gained orders from 10 air

Mirage F.1C of the French air force Escadron de Chasse EC 2/12 'Cornouaille', based at Cambrai. The unit's aircraft carry a scorpion on the right side of the fin, and a bulldog's head on the left. This particular F.1C, the 21st production aircraft, formerly served with ECTT 2/30 'Normandie-Niemen' with the code 30-MN.

Dassault-Breguet Mirage 2000

History and Notes

After the Mirage F.1 was ordered, Dassault spent much effort on the large variable-sweep Mirage G series. This led to the ACF (Avion de Combat Futur) with a wing fixed at 55°, but in December 1975 this too was cancelled. In its place came another of the small single-Atar machines, and it marked a return to the tailless delta configuration. it was, however, a totally different aircraft, designed to CCV (control-configured vehicle) technology with variable camber wings having hinged leading and trailing edges, electrically signalled controls and artificial stability. Structure was entirely new, as was the engine whose extremely low bypass ratio was designed for Mach 2 at high altitudes, calling for small frontal area, rather than for subsonic fuel economy. Choice of a single-shaft engine also greatly increased weight, the basic engine weighing 3,195 lb (1450 kg). The prototype Mirage 2000 flew on 10 March 1978 and, following successful development, production fighters were due to appear in 1983, including tandem-seat Mirage 2000B trainers. A total of 127 was expected then to be on order (48 by 1982), all in basic air-defence configuration. Despite the extremely high price, said by Egypt to be US$50 million per aircraft, the same type is also on order for Egypt (20) and India (40), and may be built under licence in both countries if negotiations are successful. Later the Mirage 2000N may be developed with airframe strengthened to fly at 690 mph (1110 km/h) at sea level (this is very slow by modern standards) and equipped with terrain-following radar and other modern attack systems.

Specification: Dassault-Breguet Mirage 2000
Origin: France
Type: fighter

Now on the point of entering French military service, the Mirage 2000 is the third generation of the Mirage fighter family. The prototype, illustrated here, made its first flight on 10 March 1978.

Armament: two 30-mm cannon each with 125 rounds; normal missile load two Super 530 AAMs inboard under wings and two Magic AAMs outboard (Mirage 2000N attack version is planned to carry the ASMP nuclear weapon)
Powerplant: one 19 840-lb (9000-kg) thrust SNECMA M53-5 afterburning bypass turbojet
Performance: maximum speed, clean at high altitude 1,460 mph (2350 km/h), range at high altitude with two tanks 1,118 miles (1480 km)
Weights: empty 16,315 lb (7400 kg); maximum take-off 36,375 lb (16500 kg)
Dimensions: span 29 ft 6 in (9.0 m); length 47 ft 1 in (14.35 m); height 17 ft 6 in (5.3 m); wing area 441.3 sq ft (41.0 m²)

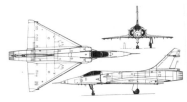

Dassault-Breguet Mirage 2000

The fourth Dassault-Breguet Mirage 2000 flying in French air force colours.

forces to the total of almost 700 aircraft, indicating that it is likely to become a successor to the Mirage III family in sales total as well as role.

Deliveries of the initial French production model, the Mirage F.1C, were made to the 30e Escadre de Chasse at Reims in December 1973, and the type is now the principal equipment of all four wings in Air Defence Command. Eighty-one Mirage F.1Cs were received, followed by 89 Mirage F.1C-200s with a fixed inflight-refuelling probe, whilst 62 reconnaissance Mirage F.1CRs are in the process of delivery to the 33e Escadre de Reconnaissance. Training requirements were met by an order for 20 Mirage F.1B two-seaters, mostly supplied to the 5e Escadre de Chasse in 1981-2.

Several export versions of the Mirage F.1 have been produced, including the Mirage F.1A which parallels the Mirage 5 in being a ground-attack model lacking nose radar. The Mirage F.1E is also

Production of the Mirage 2000 is now under way for four customers at Dassault's Bordeaux plant. The 2000C version will be equipped initially with the RDM multi-mode radar for operation by 2e Escadre of the French air force at Dijon, whilst later aircraft will have the improved RDI radar. Other orders have been received from Egypt and India, both of which are considering licence production, and from Peru.

British and European Combat Aircraft

History and Notes

Not believing in the enduring appeal of the Mirage III, Dassault sought a successor from 1961 and settled on a much larger type powered by the big TF306 augmented turbofan and flown with a delta wing, a high wing and tail (Mirage F.2) and even VTOL lift jets. The Mirage F.2 was a good aircraft but Dassault eventually, in 1965, persuaded l'Armée de l'Air to buy a similar aircraft scaled back to Atar size, and this, the Mirage F.1, first flew in 1966. Though the wing is much smaller than the delta, it is so much more efficient that, combined with 40 per cent more internal fuel in a smaller airframe, the Mirage F.1 has a much shorter field length, three times the supersonic endurance, twice the tactical radius at low levels and all-round better manoeuvrability. The F.1C reached l'Armée de l'Air squadrons in 1973, and by 1983 total Mirage F.1 orders reached over 700, almost 500 of them for export. Variants include the Mirage F.1A simplified attack, Mirage F.1B dual trainer, Mirage F.1E comprehensive all-weather attack and Mirage F.1R multi-sensor reconnaissance platform. The Mirage F.1C-200 is a

French variant with an inflight-refuelling probe. Quick scramble is enhanced by a ground truck which cools the missile seekers, radar and cockpit, heats navigation and weapon-aiming systems and shields the cockpit with a sunshade! Production is shared not only with other French companies, as with other Mirages, but with SABCA/Sonaca of Belgium, which builds the rear fuselage. Armaments Development and Production Corporation of South Africa holds a manufacturing licence.

Specification: Dassault-Breguet Mirage F.1C
Origin: France
Type: fighter/bomber
Armament: two 30-mm DEFA cannon each with 125 rounds; AAM Sidewinder/Magic rails at wingtips, plus five Alkan universal pylons for 8,818 lb (4000 kg) external stores including tanks, bombs, pods, launchers or R.530 or Super 530 AAMs, AS.30 or AS.37 ASMs or reconnaissance pod with cameras, EMI SLAR and Cyclope IR system
Powerplant: one 15,873-lb (7200-kg) thrust SNECMA Atar 9K50 afterburning turbojet
Performance: maximum speed, clean at high altitude 1,460 mph (2350 km/h), or clean at sea level 900 mph (1450 km/h); radius on a lo-lo mission with 3,520 lb (1600 kg) of weapons 400 miles (644 km)
Weights: empty 16,314 lb (7400 kg); maximum take-off 33,510 lb (15200 kg)
Dimensions: span 27 ft 6¾ in (8.4 m); length 49 ft 2½ in (15.0 m); height 14 ft 9 in (4.5 m); wing area 269.1 sq ft (25.0 m²)

This Armée de l'Air Mirage F.1C is the 68th built, and bears the coding 12-YN, indicating that it belongs to Escadron de Chasse 1/12 'Cambresis'. The 12th Fighter Wing (EC12), based at BA 103, Cambrai, was the third wing to convert to the F.1. This aircraft has the hornet of SPA89 on the left side of the fin, and the tiger's head of SPA162 on the right. As illustrated here, it is armed with two Matra Magic dogfight missiles on the wingtips and Matra 530 medium-range, radar-homing missiles on underwing pylons, and is fitted with a drop tank on the centreline station. This squadron was formed in 1952 and flew the Ouragan, Mystère IVA and Super Mystère B2.

Dassault-Breguet Mirage F.1

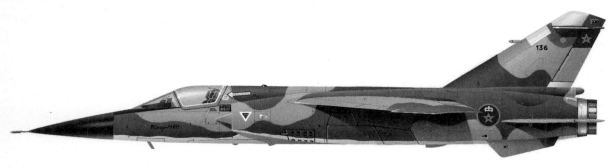

Mirage F.1CH of the Royal Moroccan air force (formally designated as the Forces Armées Royales). Morocco acquired a batch of 25 F.1CHs, which were ordered in 1975 and delivered in 1978-9. Some of these aircraft have reportedly been used in the fighting with the Polisario guerrillas for control of the western Sahara.

Dassault-Breguet Mirage F.1C

1 Glass-reinforced plastic antenna housings
2 Rear navigation light
3 IFF antenna
4 VHF 1 antenna
5 VOR/LOC antenna
6 Rudder upper hinge
7 Tailfin structure
8 UHF antenna
9 Main fin spar (machined)
10 Rudder control linkage
11 Rudder central hinge fairing
12 Rudder
13 Fin rear spar
14 VHF 2 antenna
15 Parachute release mechanism
16 Brake parachute
17 Exhaust secondary nozzle
18 Exhaust primary nozzle
19 Pneumatic nozzle actuators
20 Jet pipe mounting link
21 Fuselage aft support frame (tailplane trunnion/fin rear spar)
22 Tailplane mounting trunnion
23 Trunnion frame
24 Honeycomb trailing-edge structure
25 Multi-spar box structure
26 Ventral fin (port and starboard)
27 Elevator control rod
28 Elevator servo control unit and linkage
29 Hydraulic lines
30 Tailfin rear spar attachment
31 Rudder trim actuator
32 Rudder servo control
33 Fin leading-edge structure
34 Port tailplane
35 Main fin spar lower section
36 Spring rod
37 Servo control quadrant
38 Rudder pulley bellcranks and cables

39 Main fin spar/fuselage attachment
40 Fin root fittings
41 Sealed-sheath hydraulic line
42 Tailpipe
43 Engine fitting and removal rail
44 Inside fuel tank skin (milled structure)

45 Wingroot fairing
46 Rear lateral fuselage fuel tanks
47 Engine mounting access panel
48 Control run access panel
49 Filler/cross-feed system (rear/forward lateral fuselage fuel tanks)
50 Aileron linkage
51 Compressor bleed-air pre-cooler
52 Main wing/fuselage mounting frame
53 Wing skinning
54 Inboard flap composite-honeycomb structure
55 Flap tracks
56 Perforated spoiler panels (two)

57 Spoiler actuator
58 Wing tank fuel lines
59 Aileron trim jack
60 Aileron servo control
61 Aileron operating rod
62 Aileron inboard hinge
63 Port aileron
64 Aileron outboard hinge
65 Missile attachment points
66 Missile ignition box
67 Matra 550 Magic air-to-air missile
68 Missile adapter shoe
69 Drooping leading-edge
70 Slat hinges
71 Pylon mounting point (outboard)
72 Pylon mounting point (inboard)

73 Port inboard weapons pylon
74 Matra 530 air-to-air missile (infra-red homing head)
75 Leading-edge slat actuator
76 Forged high-tensile steel main wingroot fitting
77 IFF antenna
78 Engine duct ventilation
79 Central fuselage fuel tank
80 Aileron control rod
81 Avionics bay
82 Electrical/hydraulic leads
83 Inverted-flight accumulator
84 Amplifier
85 Main radio/electronics bay
86 Water separator and air-conditioning turbo-compressor
87 Canopy hinge
88 Canopy actuating jack

89 Martin-Baker Mk 4 ejection seat
90 Clamshell jettisonable canopy
91 Gunsight
92 One-piece cast windshield frame
93 Instrument panel
94 Control column
95 Instrument panel shroud/gunsight mounting
96 Heated, bird-strike proof windshield
97 Pitot heads
98 Radar attachment points
99 Thomson-CSF Cyrano IV fire-control radar
100 Radar scanner
101 Glass-reinforced plastic radome
102 TACAN antenna
103 Front pressure bulkhead
104 Rudder pedals
105 Aileron control bellcrank
106 Control column base
107 Elevator control bellcrank

108 Retraction jack fairing
109 Nosewheel retraction jack
110 Oleo-pneumatic shock-absorber
111 Twin nosewheels
112 Nose gear bogie
113 Guide link
114 Steering/centering jack
115 Nose gear door
116 Pilot's seat
117 Nose gear trunnion
118 Elevator linkage
119 Angled rear pressure bulkhead
120 Battery (24 volt)
121 Gun trough
122 Air intake shock-cone
123 Heat exchanger
124 Shock-cone electric motor
125 Boundary-layer bleed
126 Shock-cone guide track
127 Screw jack
128 Starboard air intake
129 DEFA cannon barrel
130 Auxiliary air intake doors
131 Starboard airbrake
132 Starboard DEFA 30-mm cannon
133 Forward fuselage integral fuel tank
134 Wingroot fillet
135 Fuel lines
136 Machined frame
137 Wing forward attachment point
138 Landing gear door actuator/linkage
139 Ammunition magazine
140 Pre-closing landing gear door (lower)

141 Main landing gear well (starboard)
142 Main wing/fuselage mounting frame
143 SNECMA Atar 9K50 turbojet
144 Main wing attachment points
145 Machined frame
146 Wing rear attachment point
147 Engine mounting trunnion
148 Inboard flap guide track
149 Flap actuator and linkage
150 Honeycomb trailing-edge structure
151 Double-slotted flaps
152 Perforated spoiler panels (two)
153 Spoiler leading-edge piano hinge
154 Multi-spar wing box tank structure
155 Pylon mounting point (inboard)

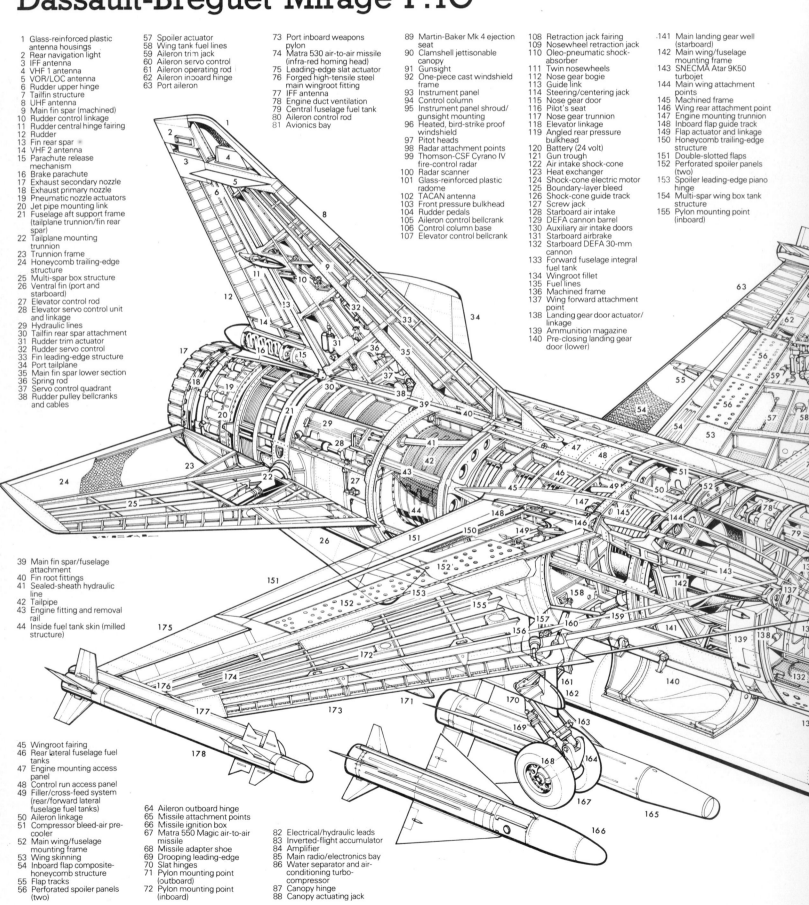

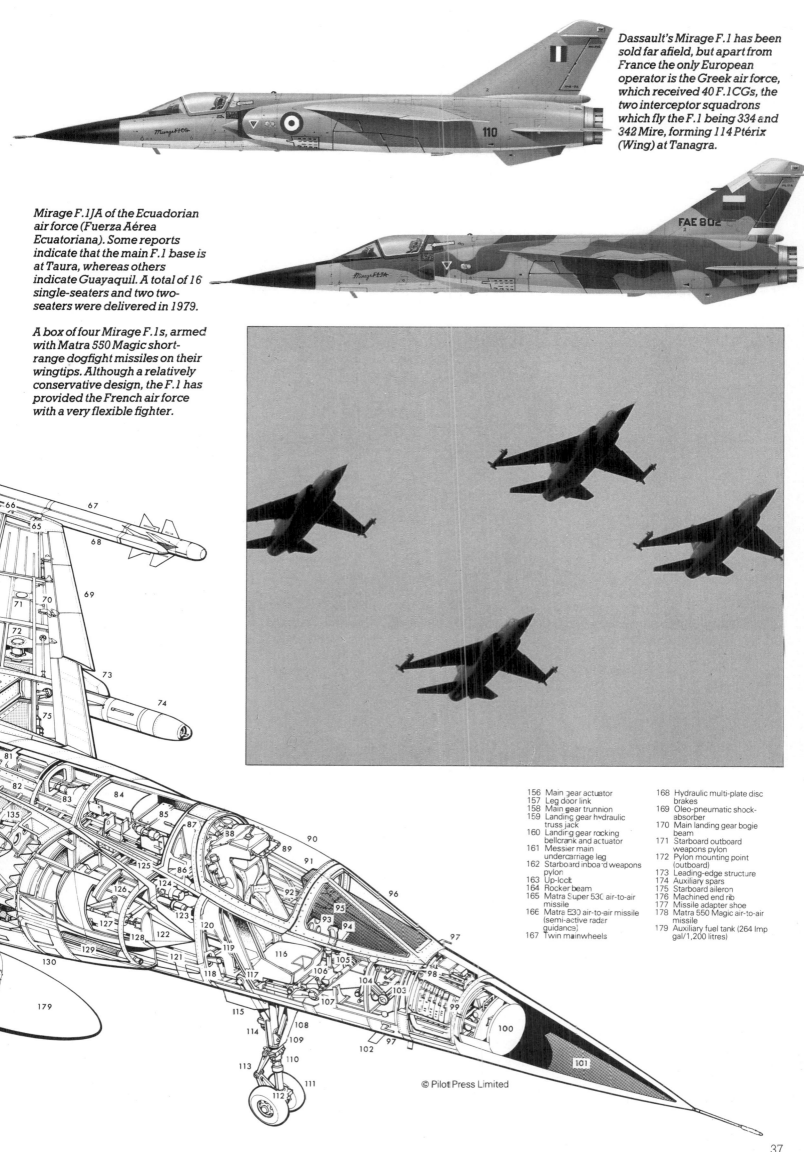

Dassault's Mirage F.1 has been sold far afield, but apart from France the only European operator is the Greek air force, which received 40 F.1CGs, the two interceptor squadrons which fly the F.1 being 334 and 342 Mire, forming 114 Ptérix (Wing) at Tanagra.

Mirage F.1JA of the Ecuadorian air force (Fuerza Aérea Ecuatoriana). Some reports indicate that the main F.1 base is at Taura, whereas others indicate Guayaquil. A total of 16 single-seaters and two two-seaters were delivered in 1979.

A box of four Mirage F.1s, armed with Matra 550 Magic short-range dogfight missiles on their wingtips. Although a relatively conservative design, the F.1 has provided the French air force with a very flexible fighter.

156 Main gear actuator
157 Leg door link
158 Main gear trunnion
159 Landing gear hydraulic truss jack
160 Landing gear rocking bellcrank and actuator
161 Messier main undercarriage leg
162 Starboard inboard weapons pylon
163 Up-lock
164 Rocker beam
165 Matra Super 530 air-to-air missile
166 Matra 530 air-to-air missile (semi-active radar guidance)
167 Twin mainwheels
168 Hydraulic multi-plate disc brakes
169 Oleo-pneumatic shock-absorber
170 Main landing gear bogie beam
171 Starboard outboard weapons pylon
172 Pylon mounting point (outboard)
173 Leading-edge structure
174 Auxiliary spars
175 Starboard aileron
176 Machined end rib
177 Missile adapter shoe
178 Matra 550 Magic air-to-air missile
179 Auxiliary fuel tank (264 Imp gal/1,200 litres)

© Pilot Press Limited

British and European Combat Aircraft

optimized for this role, but includes radar, and a reconnaissance model is also available with internal cameras (as with the Mirage F.1CR) plus the option for a belly-mounted 'Harold' pod of additional sensors. In Europe the Mirage F.1 is flown by the air forces of Greece (40 Mirage F.1Cs) and Spain (45 Mirage F.1Cs, 22 Mirage F.1Es and six Mirage F.1Bs).

Fly-by-wire

For its third generation of fighter Mirages, Dassault returned to the delta-wing configuration. The new Mirage 2000 thus produced is radically different from its predecessors despite the similar name, one of its principal features being a fly-by-wire (FBW) system in which commands to the control surfaces (rudder, ailerons, etc) are carried by electrical signals instead of the traditional push-rods. For increased combat manoeuvrability, FBW aircraft are designed to be aerodynamically unstable and are 'flown' by a computer which harmonizes the pilot's central inputs (arms and legs) into the optimum operation of each control surface.

An initial flight was made by the Mirage 2000 prototype on 10 March 1978, and a two-seat Mirage 2000B trainer followed on 11 October 1980. Naturally, the French air force was the first customer, with a requirement for 127 Mirage 2000Cs and 2000Bs, deliveries beginning in 1983. Early aircraft are fitted with RDM multi-mode radar for use by the 2e Escadre de Chasse at Dijon, the others having RDI radar optimized for interception duties. A further version, the Mirage 2000N two-seater,

The French naval air arm, Aéronavale, has recently received the last of 71 Dassault Super Etendards for re-equipment of three strike-fighter squadrons. The third aircraft off the production line (illustrated here) was the first to be delivered to an operational unit – 11 Flottille at Landivisiau, which formed in September 1978.

Dassault-Breguet Super Etendard

History and Notes
The original Dassault Etendard was designed as a light strike fighter for a NATO competition in 1957. It was developed into the Etendard IV-M carrier-based attack aircraft for the French Aéronavale, with a simple Aida range-only radar and a mix of guns and attack weapons. Dassault built 69, followed by 21 Etendard IV-P photo-reconnaissance aircraft with cameras replacing the guns. In 1973 Dassault succeeded in getting an improved version accepted as a successor, instead of the newly developed Jaguar M. The Super Etendard has a later version of the Atar engine and a completely new inertial nav/attack system produced by Sagem under US Kearfott licence, and with a proper radar and head-up display. Increased weight is matched by powered drooping wing leading edges and double-slotted flaps. Like earlier Etendards the Super Etendard can act as an inflight-refuelling tanker with an underwing buddy pack. Instead of having a removable probe it has one which retracts into a compartment above the nose. The Aéronavale cut its buy from 100 to 71 because of price increase, but another 14 were sold to Argentina, and their Exocet missiles resulted in the loss of HMS Sheffield and the Atlantic Conveyor (the missile which hit the former ship did not explode).

Specification: Dassault-Breguet Super Etendard
Origin: France
Type: carrier-based attack aircraft
Armament: two 30-mm DEFA cannon each with 125 rounds; fuselage pylons for two 551-lb (250-kg) bombs, four wing hardpoints for 882-lb (400-kg) bombs, rocket pods or Magic AAMs; alternatively one AM39 Exocet ASM under the right

Argentine navy Super Etendard 3-A-203 (indicating No. 3 Wing, Attack, No. 2 Squadron, third aircraft) was one of five operating from shore bases during the Falklands war of 1982, these carrying Exocet missiles which destroyed the British ships HMS Sheffield and Atlantic Conveyor.

wing and one 242-Imp gal (1100-litre) tank under the left wing
Powerplant: one 11,025 lb (5000 kg) SNECMA Atar 8K50 turbojet
Performance: maximum speed at low altitude, clean 748 mph (1204 km/h); radius on a hi-lo-hi mission with one AM39 and one tank 403 miles (650 km)
Weights: empty 14,220 lb (6450 kg); maximum take-off (allows maximum weapons or maximum fuel, but not both) 25,350 lb (11500 kg)
Dimensions: span 31 ft 6 in (9.6 m); length 46 ft 11½ in (14.31 m); height 12 ft 8 in (3.86m); wing area 305.7 sq ft (28.4 m²)

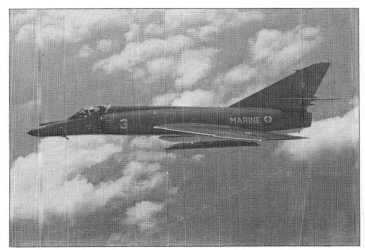

Dassault-Breguet Etendard IV-M

Dassault-Breguet Super Etendard of the French navy.

will enter service in 1986 as an all-weather interdictor armed with the ASMP nuclear stand-off weapon. Export orders have been received for the Mirage 2000 from Egypt and India (20 and 40 respectively) and both countries are considering opening local assembly lines, the latter having a requirement for 110 more aircraft. Peru ordered 26 late in 1982.

As a private venture, a 'big brother' to the Mirage 2000 has been produced by Dassault-Breguet. Sharing its advanced aerodynamic features, the Super Mirage 4000 is a scaled-up Mirage 2000 with two engines and a canard foreplane above the air intakes, the prototype flying on 9 March 1979. The aircraft is suitable for employment as a long-range interceptor and can also carry an impressive array of weapons on external pylons for use in the deep-penetration strike role. Repeated but unofficial reports have maintained that development of the Super Mirage 4000 is being partly funded by Saudi Arabia, but no orders have been forthcoming from this or any other potential customer.

France's other twin-engined Mirage dates from 17 June 1959, when the Mirage IVA nuclear bomber was flown for the first time. Four prototypes and 62 production aircraft were built to order of the Strategic Air Force Command the majority remaining in service with six squadrons. Fifteen are being modified with improved radar and other avionics to carry the new ASMP missile, and will not be retired until the late 1980s, but the other aircraft are scheduled for withdrawal in a few years' time.

Shipboard super strike

To correct the impression which may be forming that all French combat aircraft are called 'Mirage', mention should also be made of Dassault's Super Etendard shipboard fighter, a close relation of the 1950s' vintage Etendard IV. It had originally been planned for the Etendard to be replaced on the two French aircraft-carriers by a navalized Jaguar *(see International section)*, but this proposal was abandoned in favour of an extensively modified version of the existing aircraft, incorporating a more powerful engine, modern avionics, Agave radar and a revised wing. Three trials examples of the Super Etendard were produced by conversion of Etendards, the prototype flying on 28 October 1974.

The first of 71 production Super Etendards entered service with 11 Flottille of the French navy at Landivisiau in September 1978, and three squadrons are now equipped for both air defence and strike roles with two Matra Magic AAMs or Aérospatiale Exocet ASMs respectively, plus two installed 30-mm cannon. Argentina's navy is the sole export customer for the Super Etendard, and acquired 14 in 1981-2 for carrierborne service with No. 3 Wing. Using Exocets, and flying from shore bases with the aid of inflight-refuelling, they destroyed two British ships during the Falklands war of April-June 1982.

Other European Manufacturers

Many of Europe's smaller nations, whether neutralist or members of NATO, have local industries producing a wide variety of combat aircraft, ranging from armed jet trainers to some of the most sophisticated fighters to be found anywhere in the world.

The Aermacchi M.B.326 has been built in four countries, including its native Italy. In South Africa, the two-seat trainer version (illustrated here) is known as the Atlas Impala I, while the single-seat ground-attack variant is the Impala II.

This Saab AJ37 is pictured on a training sortie with the very first unit to receive the Viggen, F7 at Satenäs, whose aircraft for a long period operated in natural metal finish.

Whilst France and the UK are by far Europe's most prolific manufacturers of indigenously-designed advanced combat aircraft, many other countries are highly active in the business of producing counterparts and competitors. One of these, Sweden, is renowned as a maker of excellent-quality fighters, its strong neutralistic stance being supported by well-equipped armed forces. Local defence is based on the capability of interceptors to operate from short stretches of road if their home airfields come under attack, and thus Sweden has established a pre-eminence in combining the seemingly irreconcilable demands of high combat speed and STOL.

An early, but nevertheless effective, demonstrator of this technique is the Saab 35 Draken with its characteristic 'double-delta' wing. Flown in 1955, the Draken is now being replaced in Swedish service by the Saab JA37 Viggen, but four squadrons are expected to remain operational until about 1990. Exports of the aircraft have been restricted to two customers: Denmark, which bought 51 for strike/interceptor, reconnaissance and training in 1968; and Finland, an operator of 27, including three two-seat trainers, since 1972.

The final production version of the Saab Draken for Swedish use was the J35F, which featured an infra-red target seeker beneath the nose. Four squadrons of J35Fs are expected to remain in service until replaced by the new JAS 39 Gripen in the mid-1990s.

Saab 35 Drakens have only been sold to Finland and Denmark, the latter purchasing 20 F35 fighters, a similar number of RF 35 reconnaissance variants and 11 TF 35 trainers. All F35s, including the example illustrated, serve with No. 725 Eskadrille at Karup.

A Saab 35 Draken being prepared for a sortie during a Swedish air force exercise. The 'double-delta' wing provides a large volume for fuel, armament and equipment, and also increases air intake efficiency.

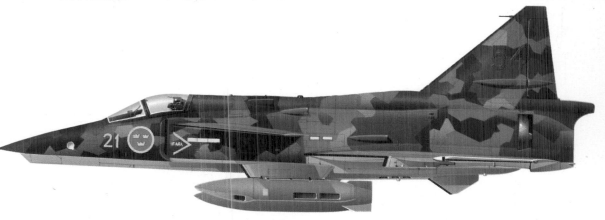

The SF37 is a specialized overland multi-sensor reconnaissance version, not normally having any offensive capability. This example, from F21 at Lůlea, is seen with a centreline drop tank, night reconnaissance pod and a Red Baron multi-sensor pod. This variant serves in F21 alongside the SH37 armed sea-surveillance model.

The first production version of Saab's unmistakable Viggen was the AJ37, its prefix indicating primary attack role with a secondary interceptor function. Six Swedish divisions (squadrons) of three flygflottiljer (wings) operate the AJ37, and in this photograph aircraft '43' is from Flygflottilj 6 at Karlsborg, whilst the remainder serve Flygflottilj 15 at Söderhamn.

For its System 37, the Swedish air force demanded of Saab a replacement for the Draken interceptor but with additional attack and reconnaissance capability. This complex requirement was again satisfied by the Viggen, an aircraft of novel design, in which a canard configuration and a fuel-efficient turbofan engine with afterburner provided excellent manoeuvrability, economical low-altitude cruising and rapid acceleration. Roadway landings were made comparatively easy by a head-up display, automatic approach speed control and thrust reversers.

The first of seven prototype Viggens took to the air on 8 February 1967, and deliveries of 110 AJ37 variants ('AJ' indicating attack role with secondary interceptor duties) began in June 1971 to Flottilj 7 (F7 or 7th Wing). Three further modes of the first-generation Viggen followed: 26 SH37 maritime surveillance and attack aircraft from June 1975; 26 SF37 camera-nosed reconnaissance variants

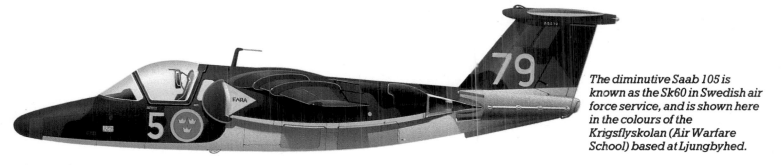

The diminutive Saab 105 is known as the Sk60 in Swedish air force service, and is shown here in the colours of the Krigsflyskolan (Air Warfare School) based at Ljungbyhed.

Saab 37 Viggen

History and Notes

Like its predecessor the Type 35 Draken, the Viggen was planned as a family of aircraft using a basically similar airframe but configured for different missions. All have a large rear delta wing with a kinked dog-tooth leading edge and a large canard foreplane with flaps. Tandem-wheel main gears and anti-skid brakes back up a thrust reverser on the extremely large augmented turbofan engine and excellent slow-flying qualities to allow no-flare landings to be made on straight stretches of country road or unpaved emergency or dispersal airstrips. The Swedish Flygvapen uses three wings of AJ37 attack aircraft as well as the SF37 armed reconnaissance and SH37 armed sea surveillance versions. The Sk37 is a dual trainer, and the taller vertical tail (with swept-back tip) introduced by this version appeared again in the ultimate Viggen, the JA37 interceptor. This has an uprated engine, modified airframe, new radar (Ericsson UAP-1023 pulse-Doppler designed for look-down interception of low-level targets, even in conditions of severe clutter or hostile ECM) and completely changed weapons, as outlined below. The first production JA37 flew on 4 November 1977, and Saab has since been delivering 149 of this sub-type with the last due in 1985. The JA37 will equip wings F13, F17 and F21, and all aircraft of this type retain considerable capability in the secondary air/ground attack role.

Specification: Saab JA37
Origin: Sweden
Type: multi-role all-weather fighter
Armament: one 30-mm Oerlikon high-velocity cannon with 140 rounds; three fuselage and four wing hardpoints for total of 13,228 lb (6000 kg) of ordnance and tanks, including normal air-to-air load of RB71 Sky Flash and RB24 Sidewinder AAMs, total of six AAMs in all
Powerplant: one 28,108-lb (12750-kg) thrust Volvo Flygmotor RM8B augmented turbofan

Performance: maximum speed, clean at high altitude just over Mach 2, or 1,320 mph (2135 km/h); radius with weapons in a lo-lo-lo mission over 311 miles (500 km)
Weights: empty not disclosed; maximum take-off 37,478 lb (17000 kg)
Dimensions: span 34 ft 9¼ in (10.6 m); length (excluding probe) 51 ft 1½ in (15.58 m); height 19 ft 4¼ in (5.9m); wing area 495.1 sq ft (46.0 m²)

Sweden's Flygvapen (air force) possibly uses the most sophisticated camouflage in the world, with four colours applied with precision. The aircraft depicted is an AJ37 of wing F7 at Satenäs.

Latest of all the Viggens, and by a fair margin the most costly, the JA37 fighter has completely different (generally new-technology) avionics and weapons, and a modified engine. It also has the extended fin of the Sk37. This JA37 is seen in service with F13 at Norrköping.

Using the same basic airframe, engines and systems as the AJ37, the Sk37 dual-control trainer has a rear cockpit for the instructor, which cuts into the tankage. Because of the extra side area the fin has been extended in height. The Sk37 can carry all the AJ37's range of weapons, and fly in the secondary attack role.

Saab JA37 Viggen

1 Dielectric nose cone
2 Radar scanner
3 Ps-46/A radar pack
4 Avionics equipment
5 Forward pressure bulkhead
6 Avionics/electronics bay
7 Screen forward fairing
8 Canopy frame windscreen de-icing
9 One-piece windscreen assembly
10 Weapons sight
11 Fixed frame
12 Pilot's control column
13 Rudder pedal assembly
14 Control linkage
15 Fuselage skin panels
16 Nosewheel bay door
17 Twin nosewheels (forward-retracting)
18 Nosewheel leg assembly
19 Nosewheel retraction strut linkage
20 Nosewheel bay
21 Nosewheel leg pivot
22 Control links/pulleys
23 Pilot's seat frame support
24 Pilot's ejection seat
25 Starboard intake lip
26 Hinged canopy
27 Headrest
28 Ejection seat guiderails/mechanism
29 Cockpit canopy hinges
30 Main fuselage fuel tank bay
31 Fuselage frame structures
32 Intake separator
33 Forward wing root fairing
34 Port intake
35 Intake duct frames
36 Low-vision light panels
37 Forward wing structure
38 Forward wing main spar
39 Fuselage/forward wing main attachment point
40 Engine oil coolers
41 Air conditioning bay
42 Radio equipment
43 Starboard forward wing
44 Flap hinge fairing
45 Honeycomb flap structure
46 Dorsal identification/recognition light
47 Cooling equipment bay
48 Cabin air outlet scoop
49 Cooling pipes
50 Coolers/blowers
51 Fuselage saddle fuel tanks
52 Forward wing aft attachment

This AJ37 in a roll emphasizes the 46 m² (almost 500 sq ft) of wing, which with the canard gives superb turn radius and slow landing. The four outer fairings for the elevon power units are extended forward into weapon pylons (inboard) and ECM (electronic countermeasures) fairings at the dogtooth kink in the leading edge.

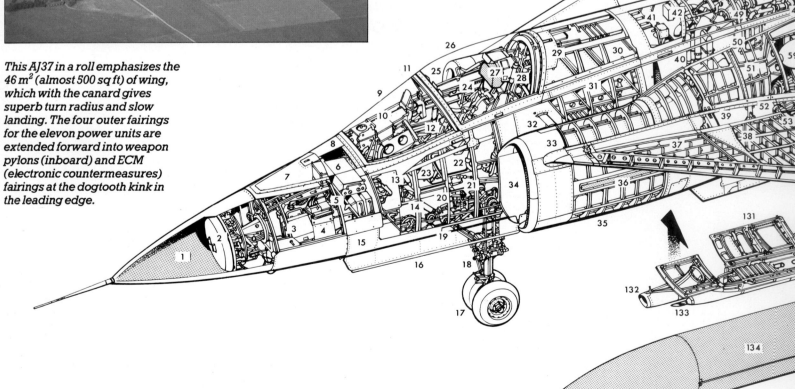

53 Avionics bay
54 Ram-air turbine
55 Forward wing flap hinge fairing
56 Honeycomb flap structure
57 Hydraulic pump
58 Low-vision light panels (2)
59 Engine intake face
60 Fuselage upper main longeron
61 Fabricated fuselage frames
62 Volvo Flygmotor RM 8B turbofan
63 Skin panels
64 Dorsal auxiliary intake/outlet panel
65 Forged/machined main fuselage/wing frame members
66 Starboard wing skinning
67 Starboard wing fuel bay
68 Starboard ECM bullet
69 Leading-edge extension
70 Starboard outer elevon hinge
71 Starboard elevon
72 Pitot tube
73 Fin leading-edge extension
74 Tailfin structure
75 Tailfin forward spar
76 Fin spar/fuselage pick-up
77 Fuel lines
78 Gearbox pre-cooler installation
79 Wing root fairing
80 Wing main spar/fuselage attachment

81 Airbrake actuating ram
82 Fuselage port airbrake
83 Engine pipe
84 Afterburner assembly
85 Thrust-reverser aperture
86 Reverser lids
87 Lid actuating ram
88 Aft fuselage frame
89 Linkage
90 Tailfin aft attachment
91 Rudder operating ram
92 Rudder post
93 Tailfin skinning
94 Tip extension
95 VHF antenna
96 Honeycomb rudder structure
97 Rudder
98 Rudder operating ram fairing
99 Blade antenna
100 Tail fairing
101 Tail fairing formers
102 Tail navigation light
103 Fuselage aft fairing
104 Tailplane exhaust
105 Inner elevon actuator fairings
106 Honeycomb elevon (inner)
107 Elevon outer fairing
108 Honeycomb elevon (outer)
109 Inner structure
110 Outboard leading-edge extension
111 Port outer weapons pylon
112 Port ECM bullet
113 Wing structure

114 Outer actuator ram
115 Inner actuator ram
116 Port wing integral fuel bay
117 Wing ribs
118 Wing skin panels
119 Inner honeycomb panels
120 Undercarriage support rib member
121 Machined wing main spar
122 Wheel well diagonal member
123 Mainwheel leg pivot
124 Mainwheel retraction strut
125 Port wheel well
126 Inboard leading-edge structure
127 Undercarriage inner door
128 Oerlikon 30-mm KCA revolver gun ventral pack
129 Ammunition feed
130 Gun support frame
131 Access panels
132 Cooling air
133 Muzzle fairing
134 Ventral auxiliary drop tank
135 Tandem mainwheels
136 Axle fork assembly
137 Torque links
138 Mainwheel oleo leg
139 Leg door
140 Wing inner weapons pylon
141 BAe Sky Flash air-to-air missile
142 AIM-9L Sidewinder air-to-air missile

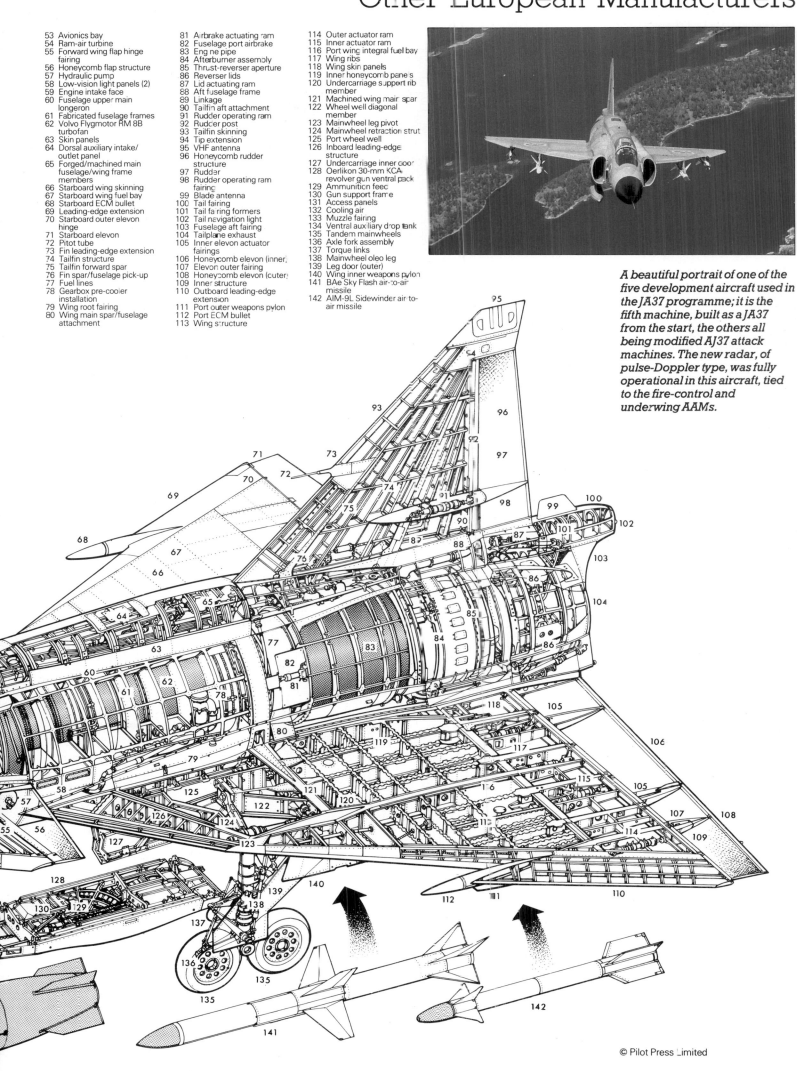

A beautiful portrait of one of the five development aircraft used in the JA37 programme; it is the fifth machine, built as a JA37 from the start, the others all being modified AJ37 attack machines. The new radar, of pulse-Doppler type, was fully operational in this aircraft, tied to the fire-control and underwing AAMs.

British and European Combat Aircraft

Of simple design and construction by today's standards, the SOKO J-1 Jastreb is the most advanced indigenous combat aircraft in service with the Yugoslav air force.

The first pre-production SOKO J-1 Jastreb aircraft is illustrated here during a visit to the Farnborough Air Show, operational aircraft being similar apart from a three-figure number on the nose, as it is not Yugoslav custom to apply squadron markings.

from May 1977; and 18 Sk37 two-seat trainers from June 1972. Improved engines and radar, plus BAeD Sky Flash AAMs, characterized the new-generation JA37 interceptor (secondary attack role), the first of 149 on order entering service with F13 in 1979.

An even more challenging requirement to replace early marks of the Viggen in the 1990s was satisfied in 1982 by the placing of a development order for the Saab 2110, otherwise known as the JAS39 (Fighter, Attack, Reconnaissance System 39). With avionics produced by a consortium of Swedish defence contractors, and aerodynamics formulated in conjunction with leading foreign aircraft manufacturers, the prototype JAS39 is due to fly in 1985-6, and will doubtless prove yet another potent Swedish combat aircraft. Initial requirements call for 140 to be produced by the year 2000, and further orders are likely to be placed.

In between its Draken and Viggen programmes, Saab developed a two-seat jet trainer or four-seat liaison aircraft, the Model 105, as a private venture, and flew a prototype on 29 June 1963. The aircraft was adopted for training by the Swedish air force and given the military designation Sk 60A, deliveries beginning to F5 in 1966. Of the 150 built, several were converted to armed Sk60B models and camera-nosed Sk60Cs, whilst the export Saab 105XT was ordered by Austria as the 105Oe, 40 being delivered from 1970 to become that country's sole front-line interceptor and strike aircraft. Two further versions, the Saab 105XH (to a Swiss requirement) and the more heavily armed Saab 105G, failed to gain production orders.

Galeb and Jastreb from Yugoslavia

Like Sweden, Yugoslavia is a European neutral despite its Communist government, the air force operating aircraft from East and West, plus a few of home design and manufacture. The principal basic trainer is the SOKO G2-A Galeb, a two-seat jet of conventional (even simplistic) layout which began flight trials in May 1961 and entered service two years later. Over 200 were built, including six for Zambia, but in 1975 the production line was reopened to accommodate a Libyan contract for 50.

A specialized light strike and reconnaissance version of the Galeb was produced from 1968 onwards as the J-1 Jastreb, featuring a more powerful engine, improved navigation and communications equipment, and provision for heavier stores on the wing attachment points. A single-seater, the Jastreb has been adopted for tactical reconnaissance as the RJ-1 Jastreb, whilst for operational conversion the evolution process was put into reverse to produce a two-seater. Up to 300 Jastrebs have been built, including six RJ-1E Jastreb export versions of the reconnaissance model for Zambia.

Italy, as a NATO member, has relied mostly on the USA and international collaborative projects for its front-line equipment, although Macchi (later Aermacchi) has produced for air force use two

A single-seat Aermacchi M.B.326K close support aircraft (right) in the markings of the Italian air force (Aeronautica Militare Italiano) test centre, the Reparto Sperimentale di Volo, at Pratica di Mare near Rome. It has tip-tanks, and carries what appear to be four 500-lb (227-kg) Mk 82 bombs on underwing pylons. It is armed with two 30-mm DEFA cannon.

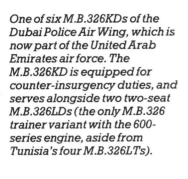

One of six M.B.326KDs of the Dubai Police Air Wing, which is now part of the United Arab Emirates air force. The M.B.326KD is equipped for counter-insurgency duties, and serves alongside two two-seat M.B.326LDs (the only M.B.326 trainer variant with the 600-series engine, aside from Tunisia's four M.B.326LTs).

EMBRAER EMB-326GB (Aermacchi designation M.B.326GG) of the Brazilian air force (Forca Aérea Brasileira). Under an agreement signed in May 1970 EMBRAER has built a total of 182 of these aircraft: 167 for domestic needs, six for Togo and nine for Paraguay.

An M.B.326GB of the Argentine navy (Comando de Aviación Naval Argentina), one of eight such aircraft employed in the pilot training role. The M.B.326GB is now augmented by 10 M.B.339s, which were delivered at the end of 1980 and also serve in the close support role, some of these aircraft having been deployed to the Falklands in 1982.

A licence-built M.B.326K Impala II of the South African Air Force's No. 4 Squadron, a unit of the Active Citizen Force, based at Lanseria. Reports suggest that production of the Impala II continues at Atlas Aircraft Corporation in the Transvaal toward a planned total of 80 units, following 151 of the two-seat M.B.326M.

History and Notes
The prototype of the Aermacchi M.B.326 jet trainer flew on 10 December 1957 and soon established a high reputation with a reliable 1,750-lb (794-kg) thrust Viper engine, tandem Martin-Baker seats and excellent performance and handling. Versions were sold all over the world, notably including South Africa where 40 were supplied from Italy and 111 armed versions made by Atlas, and Australia where 87 (RAAF) and 10 (RAN) were licence-built by CAC. Brazil was one of many to adopt the M.B.326GC made by EMBRAER as the AT-26 Xavante. Engine thrust increased to 2,500 lb (1134 kg) in early production versions and later to the figure in the specification below.

The powerful Viper 540 of 3,360-lb (1524-kg) thrust allowed weapon load to be doubled, and eventually Aermacchi produced a single-seat attack model, the M.B.326K, first flown on 22 August 1970. This has two heavy cannon in the fuselage and such add-ons as a laser ranger, bomb-delivery computer or reconnaissance pod. The M.B.326K has been sold to several air forces, and Atlas in South Africa continues producing a lower-powered (Mk 540 engine) version as the Impala II. Aeritalia continued in 1982 producing the M.B.326L two-seater with the Mk 632 engine for export customers including Dubai and Tunisia.

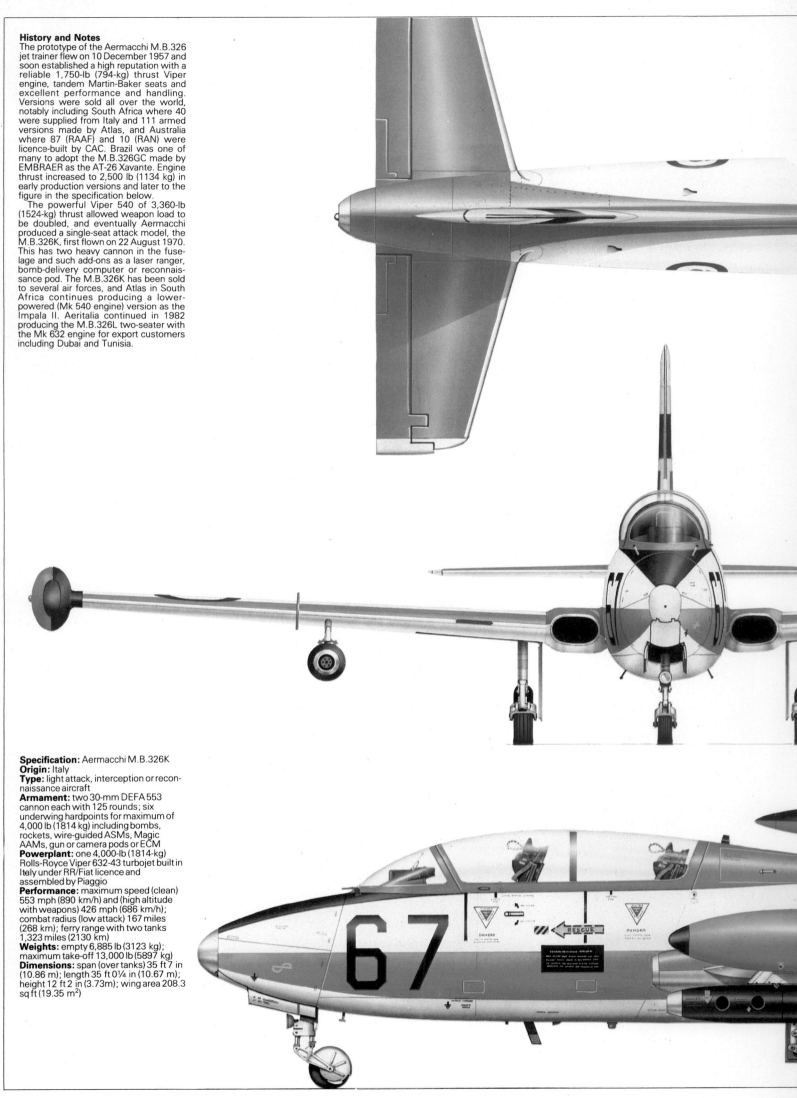

Specification: Aermacchi M.B.326K
Origin: Italy
Type: light attack, interception or reconnaissance aircraft
Armament: two 30-mm DEFA 553 cannon each with 125 rounds; six underwing hardpoints for maximum of 4,000 lb (1814 kg) including bombs, rockets, wire-guided ASMs, Magic AAMs, gun or camera pods or ECM
Powerplant: one 4,000-lb (1814-kg) Rolls-Royce Viper 632-43 turbojet built in Italy under RR/Fiat licence and assembled by Piaggio
Performance: maximum speed (clean) 553 mph (890 km/h) and (high altitude with weapons) 426 mph (686 km/h); combat radius (low attack) 167 miles (268 km); ferry range with two tanks 1,323 miles (2130 km)
Weights: empty 6,885 lb (3123 kg); maximum take-off 13,000 lb (5897 kg)
Dimensions: span (over tanks) 35 ft 7 in (10.86 m); length 35 ft 0¼ in (10.67 m); height 12 ft 2 in (3.73m); wing area 208.3 sq ft (19.35 m²)

Aermacchi M.B.326

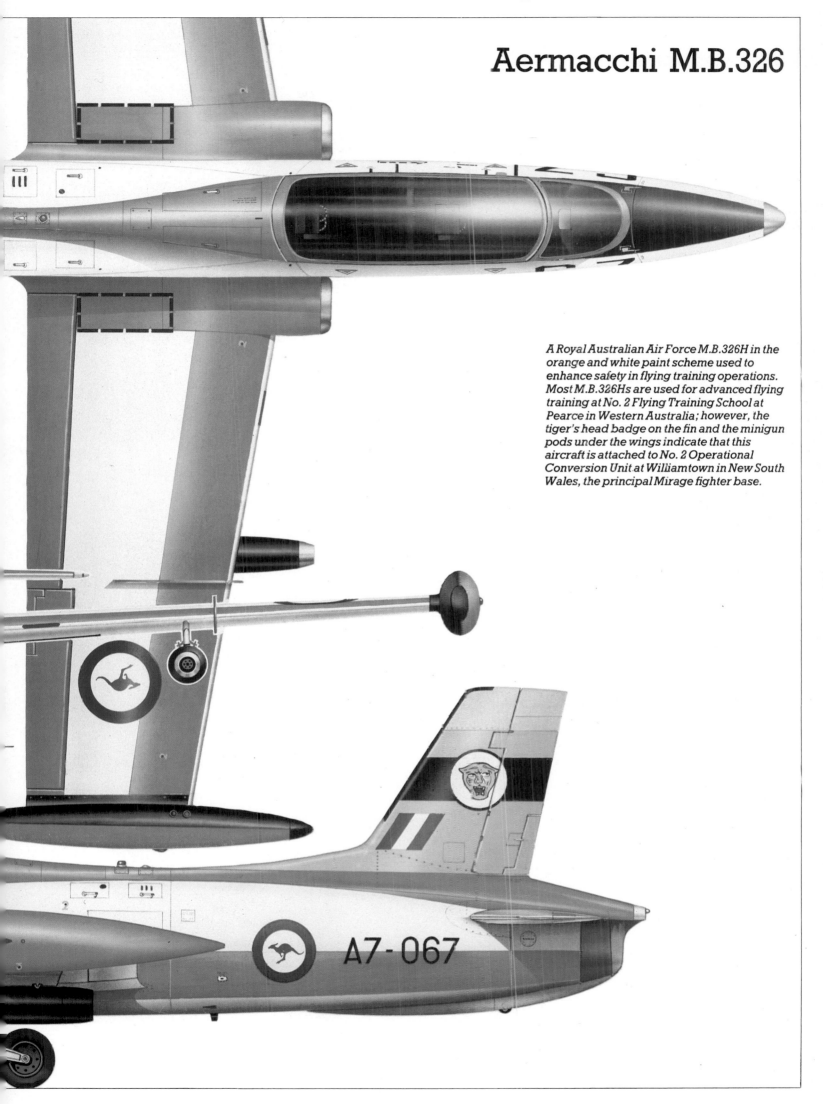

A Royal Australian Air Force M.B.326H in the orange and white paint scheme used to enhance safety in flying training operations. Most M.B.326Hs are used for advanced flying training at No. 2 Flying Training School at Pearce in Western Australia; however, the tiger's head badge on the fin and the minigun pods under the wings indicate that this aircraft is attached to No. 2 Operational Conversion Unit at Williamtown in New South Wales, the principal Mirage fighter base.

A7-067

In common with most modern training aircraft, the Aermacchi M.B.326 has been developed into a light attack aircraft. The most effective of the twin-seat models has been the M.B.326GB, here seen in the form of the AT-26 Xavante serving with the Brazilian air force.

Aermacchi M.B.326K

1 Starboard fixed wingtip tank (69.5 Imp gal/316 litre capacity)
2 Fuel filler point
3 Low-drag laminar flow (NACA 64A) wing section
4 Starboard servo-powered aileron
5 Aileron balance tab
6 Aileron control servo
7 Starboard single-slotted flap
8 Aileron control linkage
9 Dorsal antenna
10 Wing stressed skin
11 Main spar
12 Pod attachment spigots
13 Starboard central pylon
14 Wing fence
15 Starboard outer pylon (750-lb/340-kg max load)
16 Two 5-in (12.7-cm) HVAR rockets
17 Napalm tank
18 Macchi 0.5-in (12.7-mm) machine-gun pod
19 Ammunition feed
20 Ammunition box (350 rounds)

21 Starboard-hinged canopy
22 Starboard instrument console
23 Instrument panel shroud
24 Aeritalia fixed reflector sight (sighting equipment variable)
25 Curved one-piece windshield
26 Firewall/bulkhead
27 Forward armour plate (optional)
28 Nose section frames
29 Nosewheel well upper fairing
30 Nosecap
31 Nosewheel well
32 Nosewheel doors
33 Landing/taxiing light
34 Nosewheel shock-absorber
35 Nosewheel
36 Mudguard
37 Nosewheel leg
38 Nosewheel leg pivot point
39 Cockpit floor armour (optional)
40 Rudder pedals
41 Instrument panel
42 Control column

43 Underfloor control linkage
44 Martin Baker Mk 6 zero-zero rocket ejection seat
45 Ladder rest points
46 Headrest
47 Canopy breakers
48 Head armour (optional)
49 Canopy lock/unlock
50 Back armour (optional)

51 Canopy emergency jettison
52 Spent ink container
53 Control runs
54 Niche-type foothold
55 Ventral blade antenna
56 Gun port
57 Blast tube
58 Gun access door (open)
59 Port 30-mm DEFA 553 cannon
60 Ammunition box release
61 Hydraulic tank
62 Ammunition box guide-rails
63 Avionics bay (ADF IF/RF amplifier, LHF transceiver)
64 Main fuel filler cap
65 Gyro-compass compartment
66 Forward auxiliary rubber fuel tank (104 Imp gal/475 litre) capacity
67 Aft-sloping bulkhead
68 Gas escape
69 Ventral air brake
70 Port engine air intake

71 Fuselage/intake trunk cut-out
72 Control linkage
73 Main spar/fuselage attachment
74 Centre-section carry-through
75 Main fuselage rubber fuel tanks — and 81 — (258.5-Imp gal/1 175-litre capacity total)
76 Fuselage double frame
77 Avionics equipment
78 Fuel lines
79 Auxiliary fuel filler cap
80 Fuel feed
81 Aft main rubber fuel tank
82 Port engine air intake
83 Port engine air intake trunking
84 Rudder control linkage
85 Fuselage structure
86 Engine accessories bay
87 Fiat-built Rolls-Royce Viper 632-43 engine
88 Engine bay cooling louvres
89 Engine support beam
90 Engine oil tank
91 Dorsal anti-collision beacon
92 Batteries compartment (starboard side)
93 Fuselage break line
94 Firewall
95 Rear fuselage frames
96 Finroot fairing
97 Fin spar/fuselage attachment
98 Elevator linkage
99 Rudder control actuator
100 Rudder trim tab motor
101 Fin structure
102 Starboard tailplane
103 Elevator balance
104 Starboard elevator

119 Elevator torque tube
120 Exhaust
121 Tailplane spar attachment
122 Tailplane centre-section
123 Rudder linkage
124 Ventral strake/tailskid
125 Tailwheel bumper
126 Upper longeron
127 Rudder control rod
128 Fuselage double frame
129 Lower longeron
130 Fuselage skinning
131 Wingroot fairing
132 Rear auxiliary spar/fuselage attachment
133 Wheel well
134 Rear auxiliary spar
135 Port single-slotted flap
136 Wing stringers
137 'Dry' wing structure
138 Port wing fence
139 Port aileron tab
140 Aileron structure
141 Port wingtip tank (69.5-Imp gal/316-litre capacity)
142 Anti-surge baffles
143 Port navigation light
144 Wingtip tank attachment
145 SUU-11A/A 7.62-mm Minigun pod (1,500 rounds)
146 Port outer pylon (750-lb/340-kg capacity)
147 Pylon hardpoint
148 Main spar
149 Jettisonable auxiliary fuel tank (50-Imp gal/227-litre capacity)
150 Port central pylon (1,000-lb/454-kg capacity)
151 Pylon hardpoint
152 Oblique camera port
153 Quick-release catches
154 Frontal oblique camera port
155 Tactical photo-recce pod (four 70-mm Vinten 360 cameras); port inner station only
156 Pylon hardpoint
157 Port mainwheel
158 Low-pressure tyre
159 Mainwheel leg
160 Mainwheel shock-absorber
161 Leading-edge inboard ribs

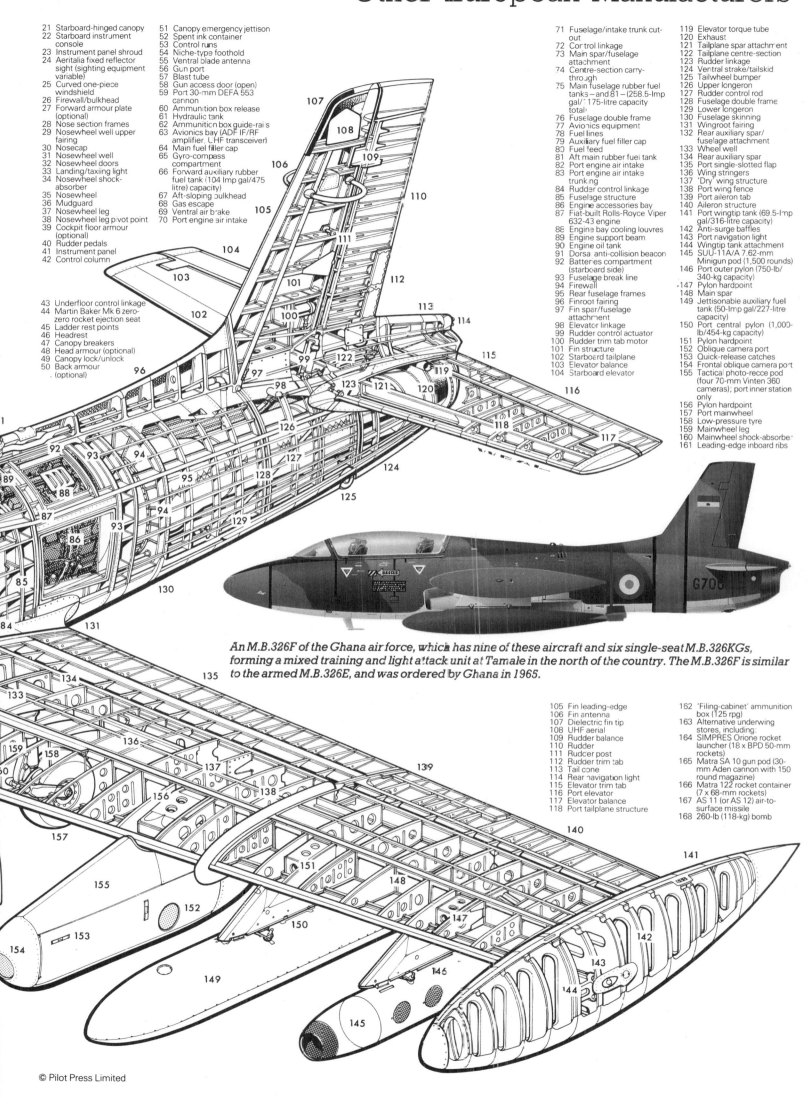

An M.B.326F of the Ghana air force, which has nine of these aircraft and six single-seat M.B.326KGs, forming a mixed training and light attack unit at Tamale in the north of the country. The M.B.326F is similar to the armed M.B.326E, and was ordered by Ghana in 1965.

105 Fin leading-edge
106 Fin antenna
107 Dielectric fin tip
108 UHF aerial
109 Rudder balance
110 Rudder
111 Rudder post
112 Rudder trim tab
113 Tail cone
114 Rear navigation light
115 Elevator trim tab
116 Port elevator
117 Elevator balance
118 Port tailplane structure

162 'Filing-cabinet' ammunition box (125 rpg)
163 Alternative underwing stores, including:
164 SIMPRES Orione rocket launcher (18 x BPD 50-mm rockets)
165 Matra SA 10 gun pod (30-mm Aden cannon with 150 round magazine)
166 Matra 122 rocket container (7 x 68-mm rockets)
167 AS 11 (or AS 12) air-to-surface missile
168 260-lb (118-kg) bomb

Aermacchi M.B.339

History and Notes

Following prolonged studies Aermacchi flew the prototype M.B.339 second-generation trainer on 12 August 1976. The chief modification compared with the M.B.326 was the redesign of the tandem cockpits to give the instructor a good view ahead over the helmet of the pupil. Directional stability was maintained by a larger fin and canted ventral fins, and standard equipment included the Viper Mk 632 engine and Mk 10F zero/zero seat. The first of 100 M.B.339A trainers for the AMI was handed over on 8 August 1979 and major contracts have been fulfilled for the Argentine navy and Peru.

On 30 May 1980 the prototype M.B.339K Veltro 2 (the original Veltro 'greyhound' was the wartime M.C.205V fighter) opened a very successful test programme for this company-funded attack version. The forward fuselage is broadly similar to that of the M.B.326K with a single-seat cockpit and two 30-mm guns below. Various customer options are offered, including numerous advanced avionic items, ECM systems, a HUD and cockpit TV display. Aermacchi has gone to particular care to demonstrate a clean structural limit of +8g/−4g and to avoid airframe fatigue or corrosion. A production batch was started in 1981 in advance of firm orders.

Specification: Aermacchi M.B.339K
Origin: Italy
Type: light attack and weapon trainer
Armament: two 30-mm DEFA 553 cannon each with 125 rounds; up to 4,000 lb (1814 kg) of stores on six underwing hardpoints
Powerplant: one 4,000-lb (1814-kg) thrust Rolls-Royce Viper 632-43 turbojet made in Italy under RR/Fiat licence and assembled by Piaggio
Performance: maximum speed at sea

One of 15-20 Italian air force M.B.339As allocated to the Frecce Tricolori aerobatic team, more formally known as the Pattuglia Acrobatica Nazionale. This special version differs from the standard production aircraft in having no tiptanks, but small tanks mounted under the wings.

level (clean but with full gun ammunition) 558mph (899 km/h); combat radius (with guns and four Mk 82 bombs, total 2,400 lb/1088 kg) 235 miles (376 km)
Weights: empty equipped 6,997 lb (3174 kg); maximum take-off 13,558 lb (6150 kg)
Dimensions: span (standard tiptanks) 35 ft 7½ in (10.86 m); length 35 ft 5 in (10.792 m); height 12 ft 9½ in (3.9 m); wing area 207.74 sq ft (19.3 m²)

Aermacchi M.B.339A

Aermacchi M.B.339K Veltro II.

trainers which have also been adopted for light strike duties abroad. First of these, the Macchi M.B.326, flew on 10 December 1957, and 131 were supplied to the Aeronautica Militare from January 1962 onwards, including six new M.B.326Es with strengthened wings for armament training. A further four M.B.326Ds were ordered by the national airline, Alitalia, for pilot training, of which three later went to the air force, and export orders of early models also included 97 M.B.326Hs mostly for local assembly in Australia. Armed variants were the M.B.326B for Tunisia and the M.B.326F for Ghana, whilst South Africa built 151 examples of the M.B.326M as the Atlas Impala I.

A higher-power engine gave rise to the M.B.326GB armed trainer, the type being built in Brazil as the EMBRAER AT-26 Xavante, as well as for export by Aermacchi. This evolved into the single-seat M.B.326K, a dedicated light strike aircraft with yet more engine thrust, and its trainer

The Aermacchi M.B.339 is essentially a development of the M.B.326 design concept with a more powerful engine, improved aerodynamics and a revised forward fuselage to raise the instructor slightly above his pupil.

The single-seat M.B.339K Veltro II (above) is a dedicated light attack derivative of the two-seat trainer, with a new front fuselage and two built-in 30-mm DEFA cannon.

Most advanced jet trainers have a secondary light strike capability, and some of the Argentine navy's 10 Aermacchi M.B.339AAs, such as the aircraft shown right, provided a convincing demonstration of their potential in May 1982 when they sank HMS Ardent during the Falklands war. Surviving Argentine M.B.339s are operated by 1ª Escuadrilla Aéronaval de Ataque at Punta del Indo, although they flew from Port Stanley during the conflict.

counterpart, the M.B.326L. The M.B.326K has weapon-sights and may also be fitted with a bombing computer and a laser rangefinder, production of 80 being additionally undertaken in South Africa with the designation Impala II. Air arms operating the M.B.326 series, some 760 of which were built, comprise those of Argentina, Australia, Brazil, Dubai, Ecuador, Ghana, Italy, Paraguay, South Africa, Togo, Tunisia, Zaire and Zambia.

It was hardly surprising that Aermacchi was chosen by the Italian air force to provide a successor to the M.B.326, this flying in prototype form on 12 August 1976 as the M.B.339. Utilizing much of its predecessor's structure with the exception of a redesigned forward fuselage, the M.B.339A was delivered to the Basic Jet Flying School at Lecce in October 1981, although five aircraft had entered service eight months earlier in the navigation aids calibration and ECM role. Home requirements are for 100 aircraft, and early examples were delivered to replace Fiat G91s of the Frecce Tricolori aerobatic team in time for the 1982 season.

Export deliveries began late in 1980 with 10 M.B.339AAs for the Argentine navy, these seeing action in the Falkland Islands war of 1982, and 16 M.B.339APs for Peru, the latter planning local production of some 50 more by Indaer. Appreciating the export potential of a single-seat version, Aermacchi flew a prototype M.B.339K Veltro II on 30 May 1980, but this purpose-built light strike aircraft has been ordered only by Peru so far.

Another famous Italian aircraft company, now part of the Aeritalia group, is Fiat, which under its original name began design of a tactical transport to NATO specifications in the early 1960s. This, the G222MCT, was intended for V/STOL operations and was fitted with banks of vertically-mounted lift-engines as well as two forward-propulsion turboprops, but when the NATO programme was

British and European Combat Aircraft

Aeritalia G222 medium tactical transport of the Dubai air force. The aircraft has provision in the fuselage for eight rockets for jet-assisted take-off (JATO), delivering an additional 3600 kg (7936 lb) thrust for take-off in overload conditions.

abandoned the Italian air force continued to support the design as the conventionally-operating G222TCM.

The first of two prototypes became airborne for the first time on 18 July 1970, and an order was placed for 44 (including 12 for ECM and other roles) just two years later. Deliveries to the 46° Stormo (46th Wing) at Pisa began in November 1978, by which time two export customers had taken delivery of their aircraft: one to Dubai in November 1976, and three to the Argentine army from March 1977. Basic transport models have also been ordered in small numbers by Nigeria, Somalia and Venezuela, although an order for 20 from Libya nearly fell through when the US government would not permit the standard T64 powerplant to be exported. The aircraft was re-engined with Rolls-Royce Tynes as the G222L and deliveries went ahead in 1980. Special versions in Italian service are the G222VS for ECM work and the G222SAMA which carries tanks of flame-retardant chemical in the hold for fighting forest fires.

By far the most widely-used of Fiat's post-war combat aircraft designs is the G91 lightweight fighter-bomber, also the product of a NATO specification. Of straightforward design and construction, the G91 made its first flight on 9 August 1956, four prototypes being followed by 30 pre-production aircraft issued to the 5° Stormo from August 1958. Many of these were later converted to G91PANs for the famous Frecce Tricolori aerobatic team. All subsequent single-seaters were equipped for light strike and reconnaissance, and comprised 25 G91R/1s, 25 G91R/1As and 50G91R/1Bs, some of which remain in service with the 2° Stormo. A two-seat advanced trainer, the G91T/1, was used from November 1964 onwards, and the last of 102 to complete G91 production was delivered in 1974.

It had originally been intended that the French, West German and Turkish air forces would also operate the G91, and although a few were painted in Greek insignia, only Germany persevered with the NATO plan. Fifty G91R/3s, a similar number of ex-Greek and Turkish G91R/4s, and 44 G91T/3 trainers were supplied by Fiat (rapidly gaining the nickname 'Gina'), whilst Dornier built another 294 G91R/3s and 22 G91T/3s under licence. Of these, 40 G91R/4s, 26 G91R/3s and 12

Looking little different from its G91R antecedent, the Aeritalia G91Y is a more versatile tactical strike and reconnaissance fighter, with better payload and performance thanks to the use of two afterburning General Electric turbojets. These are from the Italian air force's 32° Stormo flying over Brindisi.

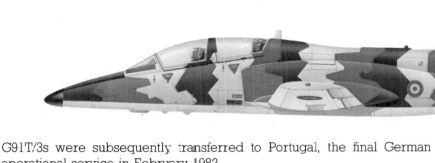

The fourth prototype CASA C.101 Aviojet was painted in a three-tone splinter camouflage pattern to emphasize the aircraft's potential in the light strike role, although the 88 produced for the Spanish air force are assigned to training duties. Those exported to Chile (where the type will later be built under licence) have been cleared for carriage of underwing rocket pods.

G91T/3s were subsequently transferred to Portugal, the final German aircraft retiring from operational service in February 1982.

A second-generation G91 was formulated by the manufacturers and gained an order for two prototypes early in 1965. Designated G91Y and known in service as the 'Yankee', the new aircraft was a radical redesign of the airframe in which the single Bristol Orpheus engine was replaced by two General Electric J85s, their combined thrust providing a 60 per cent improvement over that of the G91R, allowing additional weapons to be carried on the under-wing pylons.

First flown on 27 December 1966, the 'Yankee' was delivered to the 8° Stormo at Cervia from January 1971 onwards, and production ended with the 67th off the line. The only other unit to be equipped was the 32° Stormo at Erindisi, some of whose aircraft are assigned to anti-ship strike roles. A two-seat G91YT trainer was not placed in production.

NATO's newest member, Spain, has no great tradition of aircraft manufacture, yet in recent years has successfully exported two indigenous designs, both of which have additionally been chosen for manufacture abroad. The first, the CASA C-212 Aviocar light transport, is a rugged utility aircraft well suited to military requirements, and achieved its maiden flight on 26 March 1971. The Spanish air force has acquired 71 under the designation T.12 for transport, navigation training and survey work and a further 24 were bought by Portugal, further aircraft going to several world air arms and a small number of civilian operators. Production of the Aviocar is also undertaken in Indonesia as the Nurtanio-CASA NC-212, manufacture now concentrating on the Series 200 which incorporates higher-powered engines and structural strengthening. Over 350 have been ordered, including some equipped with search radar for SAR roles, of which nine are for Spain.

For local basic and advanced pilot training requirements, CASA produced the simple but competent C-101 Aviojet, the first of four prototypes flying on 29 June 1977. Deliveries of 88 aircraft on order began in March 1980 to the Air Academy at San Javier, the air force designation E.25 corresponding to the manufacturer's model C-101EB, although a ground-attack C-101ET with seven external stores strongpoints has also been proposed. Following delivery to Chile in 1982 of four C-101BBs with the higher-powered Dash-3 version of the Garrett TFE731 turbofan, Indaer is assembling a further eight supplied in kit form before embarking on local manufacture of 40 to 50 more. A proportion of the latter will be rocket- and 30-mm cannon-armed C-101CCs for weapons training, powered by uprated Dash 5 engines. In Chile the aircraft is known as the Indaer T-36 Halcon.

CASA Aviojets entered service with Escuadron 793 of Spain's Academia General del Aire in March 1980 in the advanced jet training role. Spanish insignia includes a black St Andrew's cross on the rudder, this recalling the markings carried by Nationalist aircraft during the Civil War.

International Programmes

The old proverb asserting that two heads are better than one is nowhere more true than in the case of modern combat aircraft design. Several European nations have joined forces with their neighbours to improve the quality and cut the cost of new aircraft programmes.

An automatic terrain-following system allows the Tornado to thread its way through mountain valleys in complete safety, thus making interception (and even detection) an extremely difficult task.

Here a SEPECAT Jaguar GR.Mk 1 of No. 20 Squadron stands outside its hardened aircraft shelter at Brüggen.

Recent years have witnessed a significant increase in the number of combat aircraft projects undertaken on an international basis, the prime reasons being the huge costs and immense research effort required to bring a programme to fruition. Nowhere is this more true than in the case of the Panavia Tornado, where a 14-year period elapsed between the development agreement and formation of the first operational squadrons; but as a low-level strike aircraft without parallel the Tornado IDS has been well worth waiting for.

Conceived in July 1968 as the MRCA (Multi-Role Combat Aircraft), the Tornado has been produced by the combined efforts of the British, West German and Italian aircraft industries in the form of BAC (later BAe), MBB and Fiat (later Aeritalia) respectively, operating for the purposes of the programme as Panavia. Originally Belgium, Canada and the Netherlands were also involved, but all dropped out at an early stage.

An RAF Tornado GR.Mk 1 in production form, with laser ranger and marked target seeker under the front fuselage. It is shown armed with eight 1,000-lb (454-kg) bombs, and fitted with two 330-Imp gal (1500-litre) tanks and two Sky Shadow ECM jamming pods.

Panavia Tornado IDS

The world's first combat aircraft to be developed by three nations jointly, to meet the requirements of four national customers (RAF, Luftwaffe, Marine-flieger and Italian AMI), the Tornado is the world's best long-range low-level inter-diction aircraft. No other aircraft combines two small and fuel-efficient engines, a crew of two with an outstandingly modern low-drag tandem cockpit, swing-wings for efficient subsonic loiter but treetop-height dash at 921 mph (1483 km/h) and the ability to carry every tactical store in the European NATO nations. Despite this, the Tornado is a relatively small aircraft, with a shorter body than the F/A-18 and a wing so much smaller that the gust response in the low high-speed attack role (at speeds 35 per cent higher than the limit for the US aircraft) is more than 10 times better. Including four of the six pre-series aircraft, the customer procurement by 1982 totalled 644: 212 for the Luftwaffe, 112 for the Marineflieger, 220 for the RAF and 100 for the AMI. These were preceded by eight prototypes and two pre-series machines, excluding which deliveries had reached over 150 by early 1983 with the Tri-National Training Establishment at RAF Cottesmore and the national weapon training units (RAF Honington and the Luftwaffe at Erding) fully equipped. Weapon-delivery trials by many methods have in numerous cases set new records for accuracy.

Specification: Panavia Tornado IDS (RAF Tornado GR.Mk 1)
Origin: Panavia GmbH (BAe/UK, MBB/Germany, Aeritalia/Italy)
Type: all-weather multi-role attack and reconnaissance aircraft
Armament: two 27-mm Mauser cannon; total of 18,000 lb (8165 kg) of disposable stores on two tandem fuselage pylons plus four swivelling wing pylons, plus centreline for multi sensor reconnaissance pod
Powerplant: two 15,800-lb (7167-kg) thrust Turbo-Union RB.199 Mk 101 (from 1983, uprated Mk 103) augmented turbofans
Performance: maximum speed, clean at high altitude 1,500 mph (2414 km/h); radius on a hi-lo-lo-hi mission with 8,000 lb/3628 kg of bombs) 863 miles (1390 km)
Weights: empty about 30,865 lb (14000 kg); maximum over 58,400 lb (26490 kg)
Dimensions: span (swept) 28 ft 2½ in (8.6 m); length 54 ft 9½ in (16.7 m); height 18 ft 8½ in (5.7 m); wing area not stated

Keith Fretwell

Tornado 9805 is shown here in the paint scheme and markings of the Bundesmarine, having formerly flown with the test serial D-9592. It is carrying four MBB Kormoran anti-shipping missiles. This aircraft was destroyed in an accident on 17 April 1980 while its crew were practising for the Hanover Air Show.

Panavia Tornado IDS

1 Pitot head
2 Radome (AEG-Telefunken)
3 Ground mapping/attack radar scanner (Texas Instruments)
4 Terrain following radar scanner (Texas Instruments)
5 Yaw vane
6 Radar processing unit
7 IFF aerial
8 Windscreen rain-repelling air duct
9 Avionics bay
10 Angle of attack probe
11 Canopy release handle
12 Port cannon port

13 Laser ranger and marked target seeker on starboard side (Ferranti)
14 Windscreen (Lucas-Rotax)
15 Instrument panel shroud
16 Cockpit bulkhead
17 Rudder pedals
18 Avionics bay
19 Cannon barrel
20 Nosewheel door
21 Flight refuelling probe (bolt-on)
22 Pilot's head-up display (Smiths)
23 Instrument panel
24 Control column
25 Engine throttles
26 Wing sweep control
27 Command and Stability Augmentation System (CSAS) controller (Marconi-Elliot)
28 Autopilot control panel (Elliot)
29 Pilot's ejection seat (Martin Baker Mk 10)
30 Port 27-mm cannon (Mauser)
31 One piece canopy, open (Kopperschmidt)

32 Rear-view mirrors
33 Canopy jettison charge
34 Navigator's instrument console
35 Port two-dimensional air intake
36 Ammunition feed to starboard cannon
37 Ammunition tank
38 Oxygen bottle
39 Nose undercarriage leg (Dowty Rotol)

40 Twin nosewheels (Dunlop)
41 Cold air inlet
42 Navigator's rear-view mirrors
43 Navigator's instrument display
44 Starboard air intake

45 Navigator's ejection seat (Martin Baker Mk 10)
46 Canopy jack
47 Air-intake ramp jacks (Liebherr Aerotechnik)
48 Formation light
49 Intake variable-area ramp doors

50 Bleed air louvres
51 Supplementary intake doors
52 Air conditioning plant (Normalair-Garrett)
53 Intake control system (Nord-Micro)
54 Intake trunking
55 Wing-root glove fairing
56 Krüger flap, extended
57 Wing pivot sealing fairing
58 Front fuselage bag fuel tank (Uniroyal)
59 Wing sweep actuator (Microtecnica)
60 Wing sweep hydraulic motor
61 Slat and flap combined motor (Microtecnical)
62 Communications aerials

Rapid development of multi-bomblet dispensers, runway-cratering munitions, delayed-action area denial munitions and other specialized attack weapons was ignored for almost 30 years. Now they are back in fashion and the Tornado IDS carries the MW-1 laterally-firing mine dispenser in Luftwaffe service.

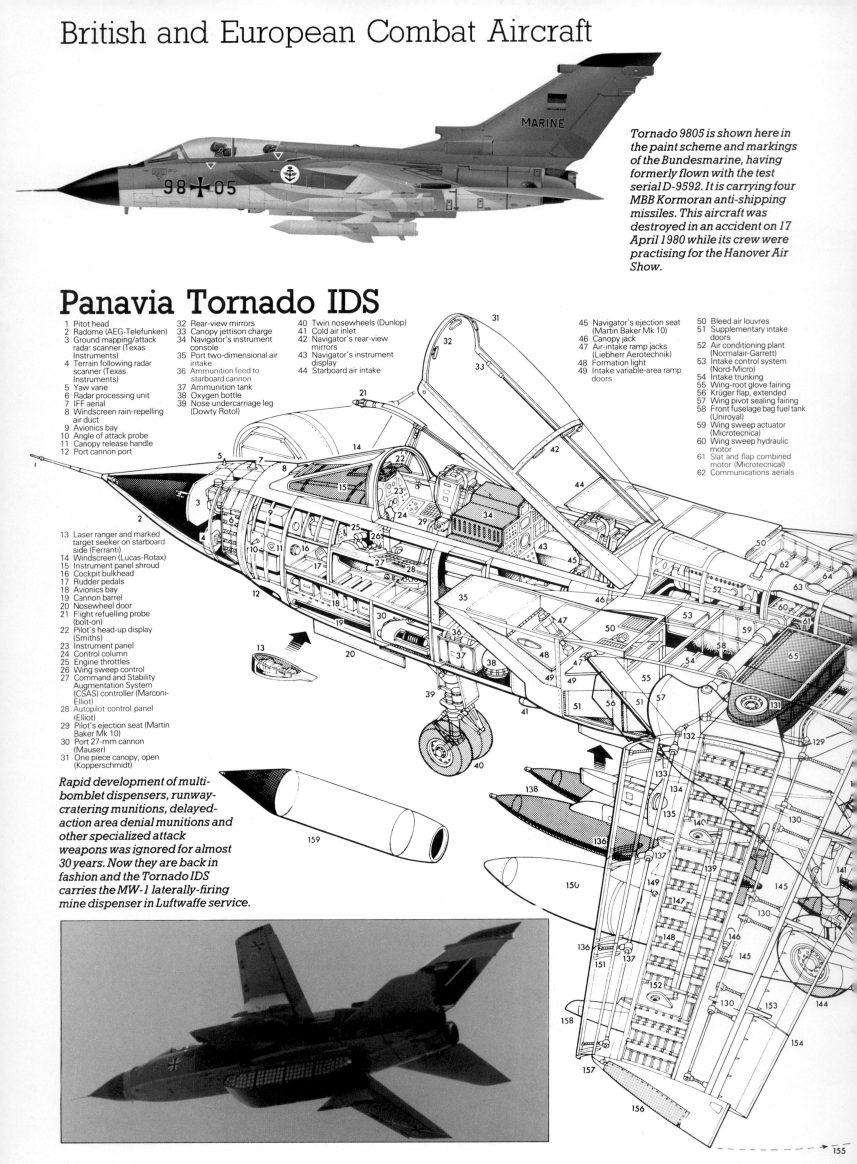

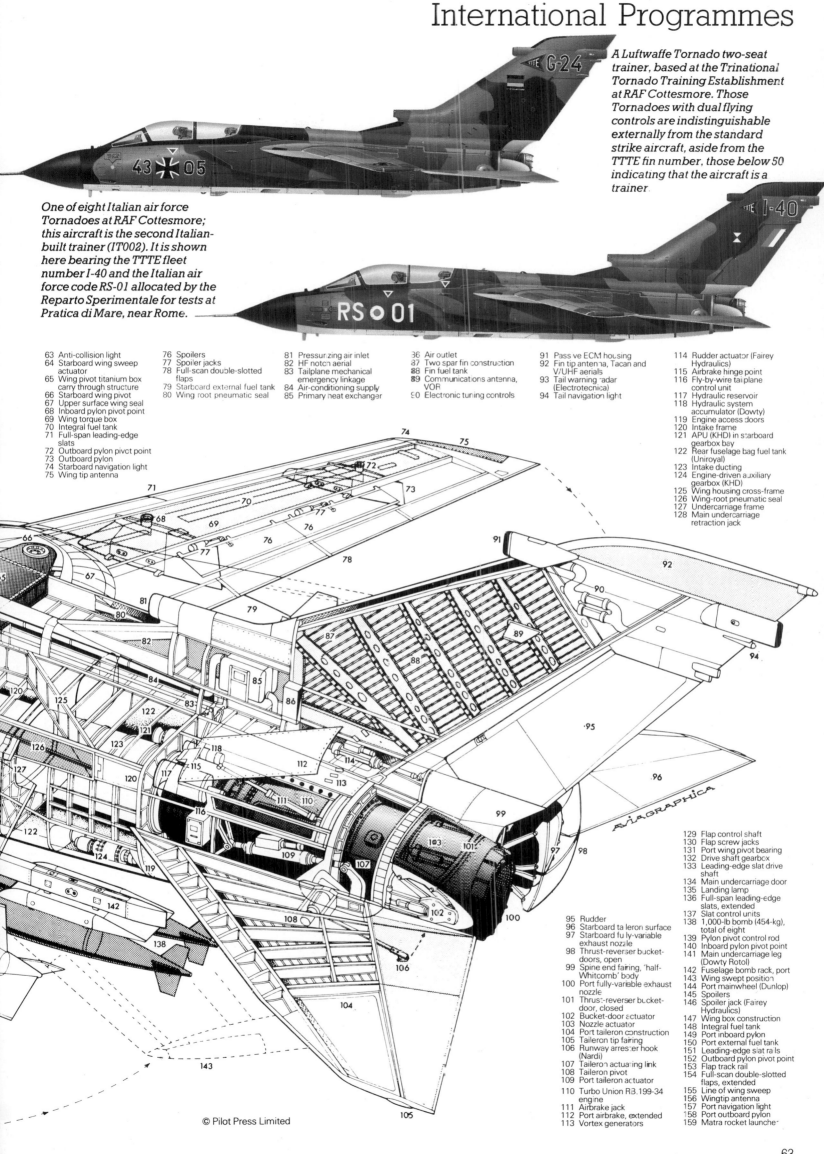

A Luftwaffe Tornado two-seat trainer, based at the Trinational Tornado Training Establishment at RAF Cottesmore. Those Tornadoes with dual flying controls are indistinguishable externally from the standard strike aircraft, aside from the TTTE fin number, those below 50 indicating that the aircraft is a trainer.

One of eight Italian air force Tornadoes at RAF Cottesmore; this aircraft is the second Italian-built trainer (IT002). It is shown here bearing the TTTE fleet number I-40 and the Italian air force code RS-01 allocated by the Reparto Sperimentale for tests at Pratica di Mare, near Rome.

63 Anti-collision light
64 Starboard wing sweep actuator
65 Wing pivot titanium box carry through structure
66 Starboard wing pivot
67 Upper surface wing seal
68 Inboard pylon pivot point
69 Wing torque box
70 Integral fuel tank
71 Full-span leading-edge slats
72 Outboard pylon pivot point
73 Outboard pylon
74 Starboard navigation light
75 Wing tip antenna

76 Spoilers
77 Spoiler jacks
78 Full-scan double-slotted flaps
79 Starboard external fuel tank
80 Wing root pneumatic seal

81 Pressurizing air inlet
82 HF notch aerial
83 Tailplane mechanical emergency linkage
84 Air-conditioning supply
85 Primary heat exchanger

86 Air outlet
87 Two spar fin construction
88 Fin fuel tank
89 Communications antenna, VOR
90 Electronic tuning controls

91 Passive ECM housing
92 Fin tip antenna, Tacan and V/UHF aerials
93 Tail warning radar (Electrotecnica)
94 Tail navigation light

114 Rudder actuator (Fairey Hydraulics)
115 Airbrake hinge point
116 Fly-by-wire tailplane control unit
117 Hydraulic reservoir
118 Hydraulic system accumulator (Dowty)
119 Engine access doors
120 Intake frame
121 APU (KHD) in starboard gearbox bay
122 Rear fuselage bag fuel tank (Uniroyal)
123 Intake ducting
124 Engine-driven auxiliary gearbox (KHD)
125 Wing housing cross-frame
126 Wing-root pneumatic seal
127 Undercarriage frame
128 Main undercarriage retraction jack

95 Rudder
96 Starboard taileron surface
97 Starboard fully-variable exhaust nozzle
98 Thrust-reverser bucket-doors, open
99 Spine end fairing, 'half-Whitcomb' body
100 Port fully-variable exhaust nozzle
101 Thrust-reverser bucket-door, closed
102 Bucket-door actuator
103 Nozzle actuator
104 Port taileron construction
105 Taileron tip fairing
106 Runway arrester hook (Nardi)
107 Taileron actuating link
108 Taileron pivot
109 Port taileron actuator
110 Turbo Union RB.199-34 engine
111 Airbrake jack
112 Port airbrake, extended
113 Vortex generators

129 Flap control shaft
130 Flap screw jacks
131 Port wing pivot bearing
132 Drive shaft gearbox
133 Leading-edge slat drive shaft
134 Main undercarriage door
135 Landing lamp
136 Full-span leading-edge slats, extended
137 Slat control units
138 1,000-lb bomb (454-kg), total of eight
139 Pylon pivot control rod
140 Inboard pylon pivot point
141 Main undercarriage leg (Dowty Rotol)
142 Fuselage bomb rack, port
143 Wing swept position
144 Port mainwheel (Dunlop)
145 Spoilers
146 Spoiler jack (Fairey Hydraulics)
147 Wing box construction
148 Integral fuel tank
149 Port inboard pylon
150 Port external fuel tank
151 Leading-edge slat rails
152 Outboard pylon pivot point
153 Flap track rail
154 Full-scan double-slotted flaps, extended
155 Line of wing sweep
156 Wingtip antenna
157 Port navigation light
158 Port outboard pylon
159 Matra rocket launcher

British and European Combat Aircraft

Remarkable ingenuity has been invested in the Tornado to enable it to meet the requirements of four air arms, not least of which was fitting the aircraft to carry the enormous range of weapons used by these services. Employing variable-geometry wings for efficient operation at all heights and speeds, the aircraft is powered by purpose-developed Turbo-Union RB.199 afterburning turbofans, and features a host of other items specially produced by the 500 European firms involved with its evolution. Though smaller than the McDonnell Douglas Phantom, the Tornado is packed with the most advanced avionics, including terrain-following radar in its IDS (Interdictor-Strike) version, and can fly itself at a constant 200 ft (91 m) above the ground at night and in the worst weather, automatically avoid hills (and even electricity pylons) to arrive exactly over a target many hundreds of miles from base. Such a mission would be impossible for any other aircraft in the world.

International share-out

The Tornado is built on assembly lines in the three Panavia member countries, these sharing manufacture of the nine prototypes and six pre-production aircraft flown between 14 August 1974 (in Germany) and 26 March 1979. Conversion training is the responsibility of the Trinational Tornado Training Establishment at RAF Cottesmore, which received its first aircraft on 1 July 1980, but pilots and navigators undertake weapons instruction in their home country. Excluding the 15 pre-series aircraft, 640 IDS Tornadoes will be built before the end of the decade, whilst four of the former will be refurbished to meet service requirements when their trials are completed.

The UK has placed orders for 220 IDS aircraft, known to the RAF as the Tornado GR.Mk 1, including some dual-control Tornado GR.Mk 1T trainers. The first operational unit, No. 9 Squadron, formed at Honington on 1 June 1982, and deliveries will shortly be made to RAF Germany for replacement of Buccaneers and Jaguars. A broad range of armaments includes the new Hunting JP 233 belly-mounted airfield-denial weapons dispenser and Sidewinder AAMs for self-defence, whilst a reconnaissance model will be introduced from 1986.

In West Germany the Marineflieger (naval air arm) has 112 Tornadoes on order, and issued the first to Marinefliegergeschwader 1 (1st Naval Air Wing) at Schleswig-Jagel on 2 July 1982. Weapons will include the MBB Kormoran anti-ship missile for operations over the Baltic, but the 212 for the Luftwaffe (German air force) are to feature the MW-1 underfuselage bomblet dispenser and Maverick ASMs, amongst others. Jagdbombergeschwader 31 (Jabo G31, or 31st Fighter-Bomber Wing) at Nörvenich is shortly to re-equip as the first Luftwaffe Tornado unit. Italy has 100 aircraft in prospect, and began conversion of the 6° Stormo at Ghedi on 27 August 1982.

In parallel with development of the Tornado IDS, the UK has been working on a version modified for long-range air-defence duties. With the military designation Tornado F.Mk 2, the ADV (Air Defence Variant) has 80 per cent commonality with the IDS, principal differences being a lengthened fuselage for additional fuel, a fully retractable inflight-refuelling probe (replacing the

NATO maritime strike potential over the Baltic was greatly enhanced from 1982 onwards when the Tornado entered service with West Germany's Marineflieger.

Panavia Tornado ADV

History and Notes

At the start of the Tornado programme it was expected t... air-combat fighting would be a role, but the dominant requirement of the customers was long-range interdiction and other surface-directed roles (though with Radpac software and changed weapons fighter capability is considerable). The RAF alone raised a requirement for a long-range all-weather interceptor to patrol the vast airspace for which the UK is responsible (from Iceland to the Baltic), replacing the Lightning and later the Phantom, and 165 are being bought for RAF Strike Command. First flown on 27 October 1979 the ADV (Air-Defence Version), designated Tornado F.Mk 2 by the RAF, has proved to have performance beyond prediction. The new Marconi/Ferranti Foxhunter radar can pick individual targets at over 115 miles (185 km) and the longer radome gives enhanced transonic acceleration. The fuselage was lengthened to accommodate tandem recessed missiles and this increases internal fuel so that in a demonstration an unrefuelled sortie was flown lasting 4 hours 30 minutes, with 2 hours 20 minutes patrol at a radius of 374 miles (602 km) with full armament. By 1982 the RAF had placed orders for 70 of the 165 required, and these enter service from 1984. Performance in all respects has been so outstanding that further customers are confidently predicted, possibly including the existing Tornado IDS users.

Specification: Panavia Tornado ADV (RAF Tornado F.Mk 2)
Origin: Panavia (BAe/UK, MBB/Germany, Aeritalia/Italy)
Type: long-range all-weather interceptor
Armament: one 27-mm Mauser gun; four Sky Flash (later AMRAAM) medium-range AAMs plus two AIM-9L

Tornado F.Mk 2 as it will be operated by the RAF in the combat air patrol role over the waters surrounding the UK. Note the absence of a cannon on the port side, and the deletion of the laser unit under the front fuselage.

Sidewinders (later short-range ASRAAM AAMs
Powerplant: two 16,000-lb (7258-kg) thrust Turbo-Union RB.199 Mk 103 augmented turbofans.
Performance: maximum speed over 1,500 mph (2414 km/h) at high altitude; patrol radius over 400 miles (644 km) with 2 hours on station plus 10 minutes of combat
Weights: not yet disclosed
Dimensions: span (swept) 28 ft 2½ in (8.6 m); length 59 ft 3 in (18.06 m); height 18 ft 8½ in (5.7 m); wing area not stated

Panavia Tornado F.Mk 2   *Panavia Tornado F.Mk 2 of the RAF.*

Tornado GR.Mk 1's 'bolt-on' unit) and a new radar, in the form of Marconi Foxhunter.

Typically, the Tornado F.Mk 2 will operate far from its home airfield and intercept intruders before they achieve landfall on the British Isles. Probably working under the control of a Nimrod AEW.Mk 3 early-warning aircraft, the Tornado F.Mk 2 will be capable of tracking targets over 115 miles (185 km) distant and destroying them at a range of 25 miles (40 km) with the four Sky Flash AAMs mounted beneath the fuselage. These advanced missiles, working in conjunction with the Foxhunter radar, are capable of intercepting hostile aircraft well above or below the Tornado's altitude, in contrast to earlier weapons.

For closer work, the Tornado F.Mk 2 carries two Sidewinder AAMs and is fitted with a Mauser 27-mm cannon (also in the IDS), although unlike some modern fighters it is not configured for dogfighting. Nevertheless, it is still a manoeuvrable interceptor, and can outpace any other combat aircraft at low level. The first of three Tornado F.Mk 2 prototypes flew on 27 October 1979, and 165 production aircraft will be issued to operational squadrons, beginning in 1986.

The three Tornado partner companies are also involved in a new programme to produce an Agile Combat Aircraft (ACA), the basic design having been developed by BAe as the private-venture P.110. Drawing on a considerable amount of Tornado technology to reduce development costs and designed around two of its RB.199 engines, the ACA was announced in September 1982 after the P.110 design had been amended in line with parallel German researches into a similar aircraft to meet the Luftwaffe's TKF 90 requirement for a Phantom replacement.

Combining the interceptor and strike roles, the ACA is to be developed to the stage of a technology demonstrator with the help of government funds, although it is quite probable that if a production version is ordered for the RAF and West Germany (and the air arms still have not been able to decide on a common ACA formula) it will possess significant changes to the design as first revealed.

Anglo-French compromise

For an earlier strike-fighter the UK collaborated with France to produce the Jaguar, an aircraft which emerged in a form very different from the original concept. The French intention had been to design a trainer with strike capability, but when an inter-government agreement merged the Breguet (later Dassault-Breguet) 121 with the BAC P.45, the resulting SEPECAT Jaguar evolved into a far more advanced aircraft able to take the front line in the strike role.

Assembly lines were set up in both countries, and the first of eight prototypes to fly was the French-built Jaguar E two-seat operational trainer, on 8 September 1968. A navalized Jaguar M was included, but not adopted by its intended customer, the French navy. Operational use of the aircraft began in May 1973 when the first of 160 single-seat Jaguar As and 40 Jaguar Es was delivered to France's 7e Escadre de Chasse at St Dizier, some of the nine squadrons now equipped using the

British and European Combat Aircraft

A Jaguar International of No. 8 Squadron of the Sultan of Oman's air force based at Thumrayt. These aircraft have been used in the ground-attack counter-insurgency role but are capable of air defence missions.

SEPECAT Jaguar two-seater in the markings of the Indian air force. India is the largest export customer for the Jaguar International, with 40 aircraft delivered direct from the UK and 76 to be assembled by Hindustan Aeronautics, and possibly another 60 aircraft to be built from scratch in India. It retains European-style camouflage.

One of 10 Jaguar International single-seaters operated by the Fuerza Aérea Ecuatoriana alongside two trainers. It is clearly based on the British 'S' version, with laser ranger and marked target seeker in the nose, and the large radar warning receiver antenna fairing on the vertical tail.

aircraft for tactical nuclear strike as well as conventional attack with bombs and Martel ASMs.

The RAF acquired 165 Jaguar GR.Mk 1s (Model 'S') and 35 Jaguar T.Mk 2 trainers (Model 'B'), early aircraft equipping a conversion unit (also in May 1973) before No. 54 Squadron formed as the first operational British unit in April 1974. RAF Jaguars are used for both strike and reconnaissance (the latter with a centreline pod), and about half the force is based in West Germany. Three additional Jaguar T.Mk 2s were also built in the UK for the training of test pilots. Using 50 per cent French parts, the UK also supplied export aircraft, known as the Jaguar International, to Ecuador (12), Oman (24) and India (40), the last-mentioned country additionally building its own Jaguars under a licence granted to Hindustan Aeronautics Ltd. Indian production will total 76, the first of which flew in March 1982.

Transformation of the Jaguar project into a front-line aircraft left France still requiring an advanced trainer, and shortly after (Dassault-)Breguet had begun work on its replacement Br 126

French air force single-seat Jaguar 'A' of EC 4/11 'Jura', based at Bordeaux. The right side of the fin bears a sphinx symbol, while the left side shows a secretary bird clutching a snake. Aircraft of EC 4/11 are armed with the laser-guided AS.30L weapon, using the Atlis II guidance pod to designate the selected target.

66

SEPECAT Jaguar

History and Notes

Developed jointly by BAC (now BAe) and Breguet (now Dassault-Breguet), who formed the SEPECAT consortium to manage the programme, the Jaguar was created to meet a need by the RAF and Armée de l'Air for a low-level all-weather attack aircraft and, especially the latter customer, advanced jet and weapons training. Slightly different versions were produced, with one or two seats, for the two original customers, and 403 aircraft of these basic four sub-types were delivered. Export sales have been the responsibility of the UK partner (often in head-on competition with the French partner) and have so far taken sales beyond 550. The Jaguar International has more powerful engines and is available with radar and other sensors, Magic AAMs and certain aerodynamic improvements which enhance air-to-air and anti-ship capability as well as giving true all-weather avionics. Orders worth £108 million were flown out to Oman and Ecuador, and Oman has placed a repeat order. India placed an order which in full will be worth over £1 billion. A substantial sale has been received from a sixth country, not yet disclosed. All versions have complete ability to operate from short grass airstrips or any good section of highway. Not least of the good results achieved has been a level of maintenance man-hours roughly one-third that demanded by previous combat aircraft.

Specification: SEPECAT Jaguar International
Origin: SEPECAT (BAe/UK, Dassault-Breguet/France)
Type: multi-role tactical attack fighter
Armament: two 30-mm Aden or DEFA cannon; seven hardpoints plus two overwing AAM pylons for total of 10,500 lb (4763 kg) of varied stores

French air force Jaguar 'A' single-seater of EC 1/7 'Provence', based at St Dizier. Note the lack of laser ranger, and the small ESM antennae on the fin. The unit marking on the left side of the fin is described as a Bayard's helmet in pale blue with white plumes. The right side bears a cross of Jerusalem on a pennant.

Powerplant: two 8,400-lb (3810-kg) thrust Rolls-Royce Turboméca Adour 811 afterburning turbofans
Performance: maximum speed at high altitude 1,090 mph (1750 km/h), and at low altitude 840 mph (1350 km/h); attack radius on a lo-lo mission 570 miles (917 km)
Weights: empty 15,432 lb (7000 kg); maximum take-off 34,612 lb (15700 kg)
Dimensions: span 28 ft 6 in (8.69 m); length (excl probe) 50 ft 11 in (15.52 m); height 16 ft 0½ in (4.89 m); wing area 260.27 sq ft (24.18 m²)

SEPECAT Jaguar GR.Mk 1

SEPECAT Jaguar 'E' trainer of the French air force.

the project was merged with Dornier's P375 in a combined bid to a Franco-German requirement. Thus was born the Alpha Jet, which made its first flight on 26 October 1963, in the French trainer, or Model E, guise. West Germany, however, required its aircraft to be produced on the Dornier assembly line as the Alpha Jet A light strike aircraft, replacing the Fiat G91.

Widespread exports

First deliveries of 175 Alpha Jet Es were made to the Fighter School at Tours in May 1979, and a similar number was supplied to three of Germany's fighter-bomber wings, beginning with JaboG 49 in January 1980, Dornier also built 12 Luftwaffe-Standard (pointed-nose) aircraft for Nigeria, all the other exports until recently being the rounded-nose French model to meet orders from Belgium (33, mostly locally assembled), Morocco (24), Ivory Coast (six), Qatar (six) and Togo (five). Egypt

Oman's principal combat aircraft is the Jaguar, of which 12 were delivered to Thumrayt in 1977-8. They have recently been armed with AIM-9P Sidewinder AAMs and will be joined by a further dozen.

Dassault-Breguet/Dornier Alpha Jet

History and Notes
Designed in the late 1960s to meet a joint Franco-German requirement for a jet trainer and light attack aircraft, the Alpha Jet was seriously delayed by the formation of a multi-national production programme for both the aircraft and its two small turbofan engines, so that though the prototype flew on 26 October 1973 the type did not enter service until five years later. The Alpha Jet has stepped tandem seats, advanced Mk 10 Martin-Baker in French and export Alpha Jets but MBB-built Stencel type in the Luftwaffe's aircraft which are used for close support and reconnaissance. The wing is mounted high, so the main landing gears retract into the fuselage into the underside of the inlet ducts. The two original partners bought 350, France having 175 of the E (Ecole, or trainer) version, and West Germany 175 of the A (Appui or attack) model. Assembly lines in France have delivered 33 to Belgium, and small numbers to other customers including Egypt which has set up its own assembly line for parts supplied from Europe. Belgium makes flaps and nosecones. The Dornier line supplied 12 ordered by Nigeria, total deliveries by 1983 accounting for almost all the 503 announced orders. Dornier is testing an Alpha Jet with a supercritical wing, and development was in 1982 centred on a more capable attack version, the Alpha Jet MS2, which Egypt expects eventually to replace all its MiG-15s and MiG-17s. The Alpha Jet MS2 is distinguished by its extended nosecone with chisel (laser) tip.

Specification: Dassault-Breguet Alpha Jet E
Origin: France/Germany
Type: basic and advanced trainer
Armament: provision for belly pod with 30-mm DEFA (Alpha Jet A 27-mm Mauser) cannon; maximum external load of 5,511 lb (2500 kg) on five stations including gun, bombs, rockets, missiles (Magic, Maverick), tanks, ECM pods or reconnaissance pod
Powerplant: two 2,976-lb (1350-kg) thrust SNECMA/Turboméca Larzac 04-C5 turbofans
Performance: maximum speed, clean at sea level 621mph (1000 km/h); radius on a lo-lo mission with four 500-lb (227-kg) bombs 264 miles (425 km)
Weights: empty 7,374 lb (3345 kg); maximum take-off 16,535 lb (7500 kg)
Dimensions: span 29 ft 10¾ in (9.11 m); length 40 ft 3¾ in (12.29 m); height 13 ft 9 in (4.19 m); wing area 188.4 sq ft (17.5 m²)

The Belgian air force Dassault-Breguet/Dornier Alpha Jet retains the rounded nose of the French aircraft for spinning training, but has four pylons instead of two and has the Martin-Baker Mk 10 seat (rather than the Mk IV) for improved comfort, easier maintenance, and zero-zero capability. It also retains the French DEFA 30-mm cannon. This first aircraft was completed in France, making its maiden flight on 20 June 1978 at Toulouse, whereas the remainder of the 33 Belgian aircraft were assembled by SABCA at Gosselies. The Alpha Jet replaced the T-33 and Fouga Magister at the Ecole de Pilotage Avancée at Brustem/St Trond in 1979-80.

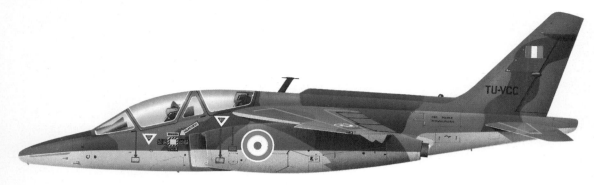

One of six Alpha Jets of the Force Aérienne de Côte d'Ivoire, which were ordered in September 1977 and delivered in late 1980 and early 1981. The original order reportedly covered 12 aircraft, but was later halved, making Alpha Jets available for early delivery to Qatar. These six aircraft are the country's only combat element.

Although painted in French air force camouflage and bearing French roundels, this Alpha Jet is distinguishable as an export aircraft by its enlarged dorsal fairing (reportedly housing an HF antenna) and its four pylons.

Dassault-Breguet/ Dornier Alpha Jet E

1 Nose cone
2 Nosewheel bay bulkhead
3 Fixed nose strake
4 Nose undercarriage wheel bay
5 Nosewheel door mechanism
6 Temperature probe
7 Fresh air intake
8 Nose undercarriage leg strut
9 Pivoted axle beam
10 Spray suppression nosewheel tyre
11 Pitot tube
12 Nosewheel leg door
13 Nosewheel pivot fixing
14 Oxygen filler point
15 Liquid oxygen container
16 Cockpit front pressure bulkhead
17 Rudder pedals
18 Rudder pedal access panel
19 Footboards
20 Control column linkage
21 Rudder cable run
22 Cockpit coaming

23 Instrument panel shroud
24 Windscreen panels
25 Pilot's head-up display (navigational data display on trainer version)
26 Starboard side console panel
27 Control column
28 Canopy latch
29 Engine throttle levers
30 Front seat boarding step
31 Aileron control rod run

32 Port side console panel
33 Seat/parachute harness
34 Student pilot's Martin Baker AJRM-4 ejection seat
35 Ejection seat headrest
36 Face blind firing handle
37 Canopy breaker arms
38 Forward hinged canopy
39 Canopy operating jack
40 Rear cockpit blast shield
41 Ejection seat launch rails
42 Rear rudder pedal linkages
43 Canopy emergency release handle
44 SFIM 550 inertial platform
45 Rear cockpit elevated floor level

46 Boundary layer splitter plate
47 Port engine air intake
48 Forward avionics equipment bay
49 Intake duct framing
50 Splitter plate honeycomb construction
51 Boarding step
52 Rear seat throttle levers
53 Boundary layer spill duct
54 Rear canopy latch
55 Rear instrument panel shroud
56 Canopy centre section glazing
57 Fixed canopy arch

58 Rear pilot/instructor's ejection seat
59 Rear hinged canopy cover
60 Ejection seat headrest
61 Cockpit rear pressure bulkhead
62 Canopy hinges
63 Control rod runs
64 Wing leading edge fairing
65 Wing centre section carry through
66 Skin panel bolted joint strap
67 Central flap hydraulic jack
68 Electrical cable ducting
69 Dorsal spine fairing
70 UHF aerial
71 Starboard wing panel bolted joint

72 Wing skin panel spanwise joint
73 Starboard wing integral fuel tank, total internal fuel capacity 418 Imp gal (1900 litres)
74 Compound sweep leading edge section
75 Inboard pylon hardpoint
76 68.2 Imp gal (310 litres) auxiliary fuel tank
77 Tank filler cap
78 Outboard tank pylon
79 Leading edge dog-tooth
80 Fuel system access panels
81 Starboard navigation light
82 Wing tip fairing
83 Starboard aileron
84 Static dischargers
85 Aileron control linkage
86 Hydraulic operating jack
87 Aileron push-pull rod
88 Flap hinge fairings
89 Flap vane
90 Starboard double-slotted Fowler-type flap
91 Inboard flap guide rail
92 Control system mechanical mixer unit
93 Flap operating mechanism
94 Rear spar
95 Rear fuselage fuel tank
96 Fixed trailing edge fillet
97 Fuel filler cap
98 Air conditioning plant

99 Dorsal spine access panels
100 Heat exchanger fresh air scoop
101 Tailplane control runs
102 Starboard airbrake, open position
103 Anti-collision light
104 Rudder control cables
105 Fin root fairing
106 Starboard tailplane
107 Tailfin construction
108 Fin main spar
109 VOR aerial
110 VHF/UHF combined aerial
111 Dielectric fin tip aerial fairing
112 TACAN aerial
113 Static dischargers
114 Rudder construction
115 Rudder hinge control
116 Rudder operating jack
117 Tailcone
118 Crash recorder
119 Tail navigation light
120 Port all-flying tailplane construction
121 Tailplane spar box
122 Pivot fixing
123 Tailcone/fin attachment mainframe
124 Tailplane hydraulic jack
125 Pilot's personal equipment/baggage locker, door on starboard side

126 Port airbrake
127 Airbrake hydraulic jack
128 Rear avionics bay
129 Airbrake hinge fixing
130 Radio equipment bay
131 Battery
132 Engine tailcone fairing
133 Exhaust nozzle
134 Fan air duct
135 Tailpipe, hot stream exhaust
136 SNECMA/Turboméca Larzac 04-C5 turbofan engine
137 Engine bay ventilating air schoop
138 Engine bay bulkhead
139 Intake compressor face
140 Engine accessory gearbox

141 Engine bay access doors
142 Port wing inboard pylon hardpoint
143 Front spar
144 Wing rib construction
145 Machined wing skin/stringer panel
146 Port wing integral fuel tank
147 Flap shroud fairing

148 Flap rib construction
149 Port double-slotted Fowler-type flap
150 Aileron hydraulic jack
151 Port aileron construction
152 Static dischargers
153 Glassfibre honeycomb wing tip fairing
154 Wing tip jacking point
155 Port navigation light
156 Port 68.2 Imp gal (310 litres) external fuel tank
157 Fuel filler cap
158 Tank pylon
159 Pylon attachment spigot
160 Wing leading-edge rib construction
161 Outboard pylon hardpoint
162 Leading edge dog-tooth
163 Port mainwheel
164 Pivoted axle beam
165 Landing/taxiing lamp
166 Shock absorber strut
167 Mainwheel leg door
168 Ground connections panel, electrical, hydraulic and intercom
169 Main undercarriage leg pivot fixing
170 Hydraulic retraction jack
171 Hydraulic downlock strut
172 Mainwheel door
173 Main undercarriage wheel bay
174 Intake duct framing

175 Intake trunking
176 Centre fuselage bag-type fuel tank
177 Rear seat boarding steps
178 Position of pressure refuelling connection (actually located on starboard side)
179 Fuselage jacking point

AVIAGRAPHICA

© Pilot Press Limited

An Alpha Jet of the Patrouille Aérobatique de France (PAF), which is based at the Ecole de l'Air at Salon de Provence, the French air force equivalent of the RAF College at Cranwell.

British and European Combat Aircraft

Morocco was the fourth export customer for the Alpha Jet, a contract for 24 aircraft being signed in February 1978, and deliveries commencing late in the following year (the first aircraft being the 36th built).

The 26th French air force Alpha Jet (E26) in the marking of Groupement Ecole 314, based at Tours. The fin marking combining a stork and a star derives from the unit's origins in Morocco in 1943, when it was a fighter school based on GCI 1/2 'Cigognes'. The unit moved to France in 1971 with T-33s and Mystère IVAs.

Togo was the second export customer for the Alpha Jet, ordering five aircraft for the Force Aérienne Togolaise in May 1977, delivery taking place in 1981. Student pilots come to the Alpha Jet from the Magister. The Alpha Jets can also be used for light attack duties, alongside six EMBRAER EMB.326GCs.

The Alpha Jets of the Luftwaffe have a light ground attack role. A total of 175 was delivered, equipping JaboG 41 at Husum, JaboG 43 at Oldenburg, JaboG 49 at Fürstenfeldbruck and the weapons-training unit at Beja in Portugal.

French air force Alpha Jets of the Patrouille de France aerobatic team, that nation's equivalent of the RAF Red Arrows. Alpha Jets took over from the obsolescent Fouga Magister late in 1980.

also bought 30, of which 26 were locally built at Helwan and delivered from October 1982.

A new version of the aircraft has also been ordered by Egypt (15) and Cameroun (six) in the form of the strike-dedicated Alpha Jet MS2, the trainer retrospectively becoming the MS1. In the Alpha Jet MS2 improved weapons delivery and navigation capability is imparted by additional avionics, the most apparent of which is a laser rangefinder in a 'sawn-off' nose.

Dassault-Breguet is also responsible for Europe's sole indigenous turboprop maritime patrol aircraft, the Atlantic, which was produced to a NATO specification and first flown on 21 October 1961. The aircraft entered service simultaneously with the French and German navies in December 1965 against orders for 40 and 20 respectively, and was built for the Netherlands (nine) and Italy (18), Pakistan also acquiring three ex-French aircraft. In 1982, 42 Atlantic G2 (Génération Deux, or Second Generation) aircraft were ordered for the French navy, incorporating improved constructional techniques and a comprehensive refit with more modern avionics. The aircraft, due for delivery from 1987 onwards, are externally distinguishable from their predecessors through fitments such as a chin-mounted infra-red TV camera and wing-tip ESM pods.

The first of three French Aéronavale Atlantics sold in 1975 to the Pakistan navy and operated for a time from Karachi. Reports suggest that the Atlantics have now been returned to France, possibly because they required too much skilled manpower.

A rarely-illustrated electronic intelligence (Elint) version of the West German Bundesmarine Atlantic. Note the ventral radome and extra blade antenna.

The Dassault-Breguet Atlantic maritime patrol aircraft has been built for four NATO members (and additionally supplied to Pakistan), but in its advanced form as the Atlantic G2 – the aerodynamic prototype of which is illustrated here – it has only secured a contract from the French navy.

Dassault-Breguet Atlantic

History and Notes

The Atlantic stemmed from the Breguet Br 1150, the winning design in a 1958 NATO contest for a new maritime patrol aircraft to succeed the P-2 Neptune. Though the choice was approved by all 15 NATO members in December 1958, and ordered into production by a multinational consortium called SECBAT, the Atlantic was bought by only a few countries, notably excluding the UK and the USA, and Belgium whose industry had a major share in SECBAT. Other partners, apart from the parent firm, were Sud-Aviation, Dornier and Fokker. Italy joined after placing an order, and the British engines and propellers were likewise shared out among participating nations. The prototype flew on 21 October 1961 and deliveries began in December 1965, totalling 87 for France (37), West Germany (20), Italy (18), Netherlands (9) and Pakistan (3). Skinned largely with aluminium honeycomb sandwich, the Atlantic has a capacious double-bubble section fuselage and efficient long-span wing, and comprehensive avionics managed by a crew of 12. Five German machines are ECM platforms. On 8 May 1981 Dassault-Breguet flew the first ANG (Atlantic Nouvelle Génération) with completely updated avionics and improved structure. France expects to buy 42 ANGs (now the G2) made by the same SECBAT consortium, and other orders are being sought.

Specification: Dassault-Breguet Atlantic G2
Origin: multi-national to French design
Type: maritime patrol and ASW aircraft
Armament: unpressurized weapon bay houses all NATO bombs, torpedoes (8), depth charges, mines and missiles, a typical load being one AM39 Exocet plus three AS torpedoes; four wing pylons for 7,716 lb (3500 kg) of stores including pods, containers, rockets or ASMs
Powerplant: two 6,220-ehp (4703-ekW) Rolls-Royce Tyne 21 turboprops made by multi-national group
Performance: maximum speed at sea level 368 mph (592 km/h), and at 20,000 ft (6905 m) 409 mph (658 km/h); range 5,065 miles (8150 km); endurance 18 hours
Weights: empty 55,775 lb (25300 kg); maximum take-off 101,850 lb (46200 kg)
Dimensions: span (over ESM pods) 122 ft 4½ in (37.3 m); length 107 ft 0¼ in (32.62 m); height 37 ft 3 in (11.35 m); wing area 1,295.3 sq ft (120.34 m²)

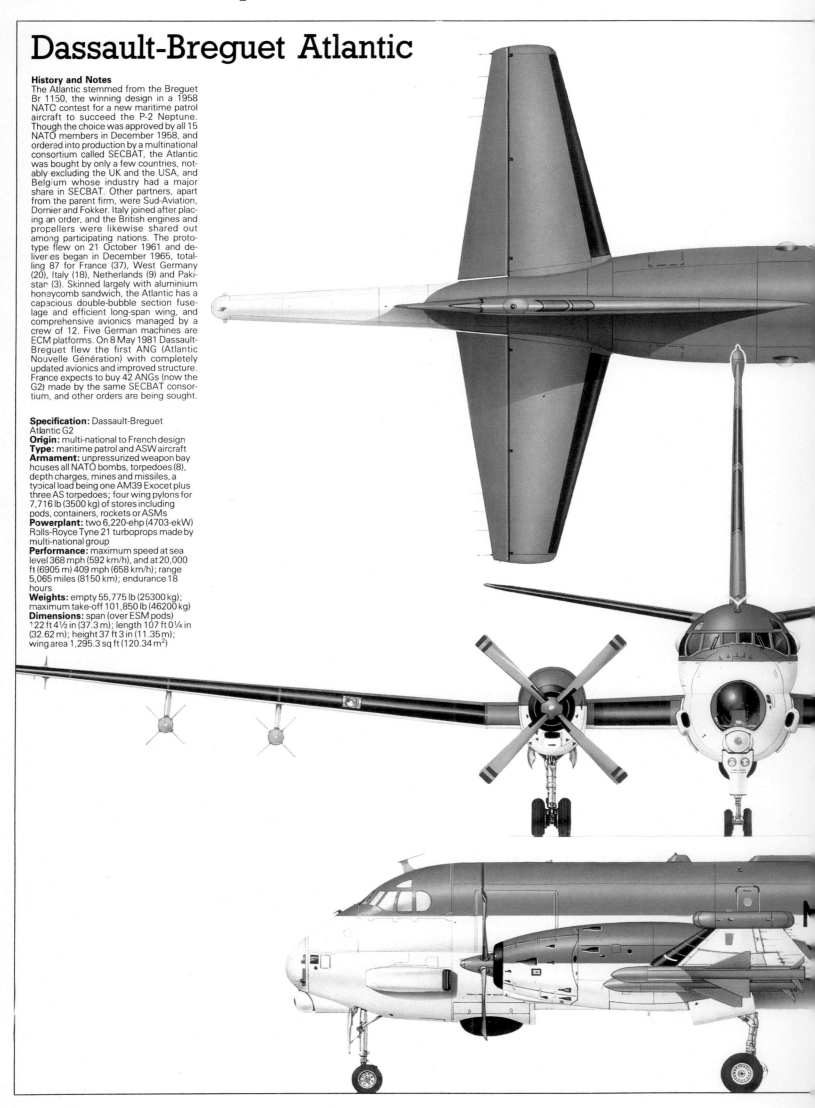

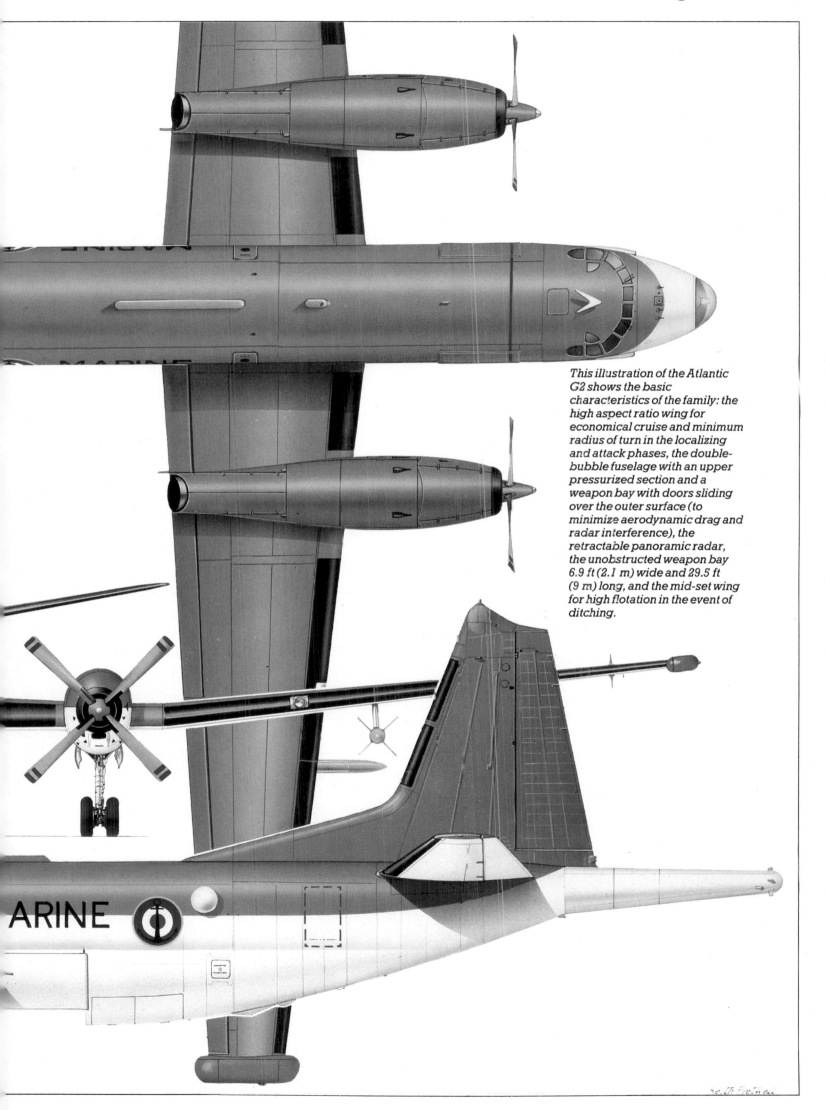

This illustration of the Atlantic G2 shows the basic characteristics of the family: the high aspect ratio wing for economical cruise and minimum radius of turn in the localizing and attack phases, the double-bubble fuselage with an upper pressurized section and a weapon bay with doors sliding over the outer surface (to minimize aerodynamic drag and radar interference), the retractable panoramic radar, the unobstructed weapon bay 6.9 ft (2.1 m) wide and 29.5 ft (9 m) long, and the mid-set wing for high flotation in the event of ditching.

Dassault-Breguet Atlantic G2

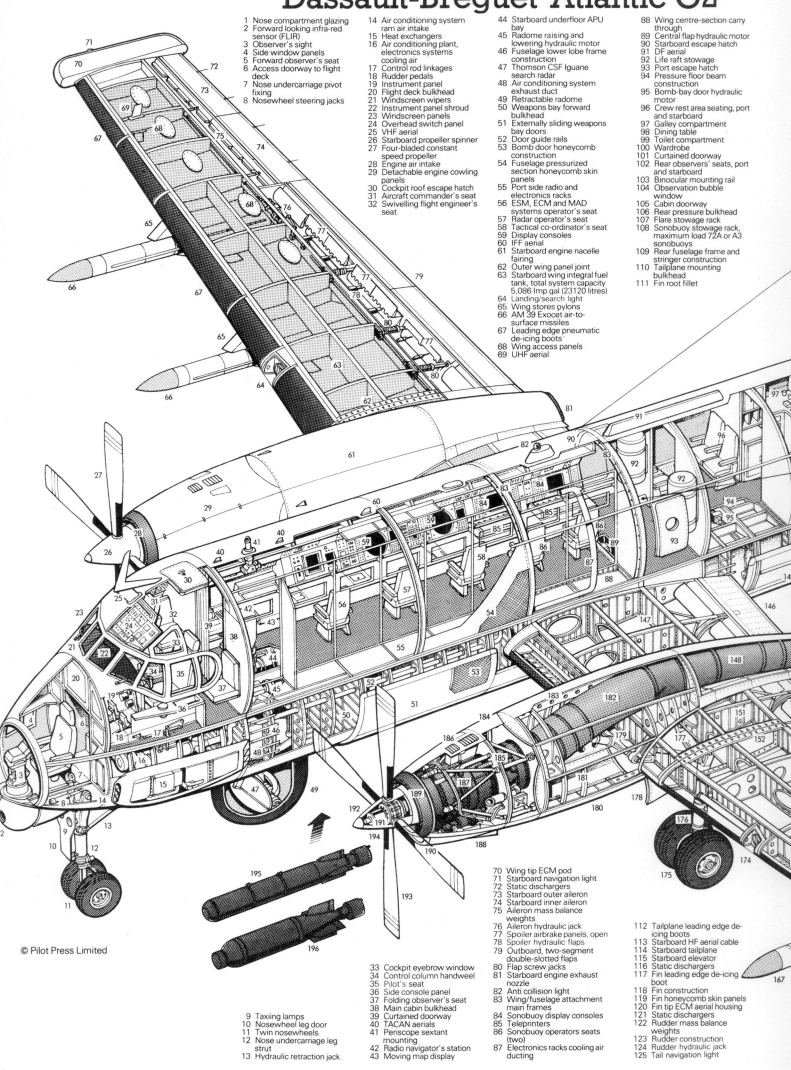

1 Nose compartment glazing
2 Forward looking infra-red sensor (FLIR)
3 Observer's sight
4 Side window panels
5 Forward observer's seat
6 Access doorway to flight deck
7 Nose undercarriage pivot fixing
8 Nosewheel steering jacks

9 Taxiing lamps
10 Nosewheel leg door
11 Twin nosewheels
12 Nose undercarriage leg strut
13 Hydraulic retraction jack

14 Air conditioning system ram air intake
15 Heat exchangers
16 Air conditioning plant, electronics systems cooling air
17 Control rod linkages
18 Rudder pedals
19 Instrument panel
20 Flight deck bulkhead
21 Windscreen wipers
22 Instrument panel shroud
23 Windscreen panels
24 Overhead switch panel
25 VHF aerial
26 Starboard propeller spinner
27 Four-bladed constant speed propeller
28 Engine air intake
29 Detachable engine cowling panels
30 Cockpit roof escape hatch
31 Aircraft commander's seat
32 Swivelling flight engineer's seat

33 Cockpit eyebrow window
34 Control column handwheel
35 Pilot's seat
36 Side console panel
37 Folding observer's seat
38 Main cabin bulkhead
39 Curtained doorway
40 TACAN aerials
41 Periscope sextant mounting
42 Radio navigator's station
43 Moving map display

44 Starboard underfloor APU bay
45 Radome raising and lowering hydraulic motor
46 Fuselage lower lobe frame construction
47 Thomson CSF Iguane search radar
48 Air conditioning system exhaust duct
49 Retractable radome
50 Weapons bay forward bulkhead
51 Externally sliding weapons bay doors
52 Door guide rails
53 Bomb door honeycomb construction
54 Fuselage pressurized section honeycomb skin panels
55 Port side radio and electronics racks
56 ESM, ECM and MAD systems operator's seat
57 Radar operator's seat
58 Tactical co-ordinator's seat
59 Display consoles
60 IFF aerial
61 Starboard engine nacelle fairing
62 Outer wing panel joint
63 Starboard wing integral fuel tank, total system capacity 5,086 Imp gal (23120 litres)
64 Landing/search light
65 Wing stores pylons
66 AM 39 Exocet air-to-surface missiles
67 Leading edge pneumatic de-icing boots
68 Wing access panels
69 UHF aerial

70 Wing tip ECM pod
71 Starboard navigation light
72 Static dischargers
73 Starboard outer aileron
74 Starboard inner aileron
75 Aileron mass balance weights
76 Aileron hydraulic jack
77 Spoiler airbrake panels, open
78 Spoiler hydraulic flaps
79 Outboard, two-segment double-slotted flaps
80 Flap screw jacks
81 Starboard engine exhaust nozzle
82 Anti collision light
83 Wing/fuselage attachment main frames
84 Sonobuoy display consoles
85 Teleprinters
86 Sonobuoy operators seats (two)
87 Electronics racks cooling air ducting

88 Wing centre-section carry through
89 Central flap hydraulic motor
90 Starboard escape hatch
91 DF aerial
92 Life raft stowage
93 Port escape hatch
94 Pressure floor beam construction
95 Bomb-bay door hydraulic motor
96 Crew rest area seating, port and starboard
97 Galley compartment
98 Dining table
99 Toilet compartment
100 Wardrobe
101 Curtained doorway
102 Rear observers' seats, port and starboard
103 Binocular mounting rail
104 Observation bubble window
105 Cabin doorway
106 Rear pressure bulkhead
107 Flare stowage rack
108 Sonobuoy stowage rack, maximum load 72A or A3 sonobuoys
109 Rear fuselage frame and stringer construction
110 Tailplane mounting bulkhead
111 Fin root fillet

112 Tailplane leading edge de-icing boots
113 Starboard HF aerial cable
114 Starboard tailplane
115 Starboard elevator
116 Static dischargers
117 Fin leading edge de-icing boot
118 Fin construction
119 Fin honeycomb skin panels
120 Fin tip ECM aerial housing
121 Static dischargers
122 Rudder mass balance weights
123 Rudder construction
124 Rudder hydraulic jack
125 Tail navigation light

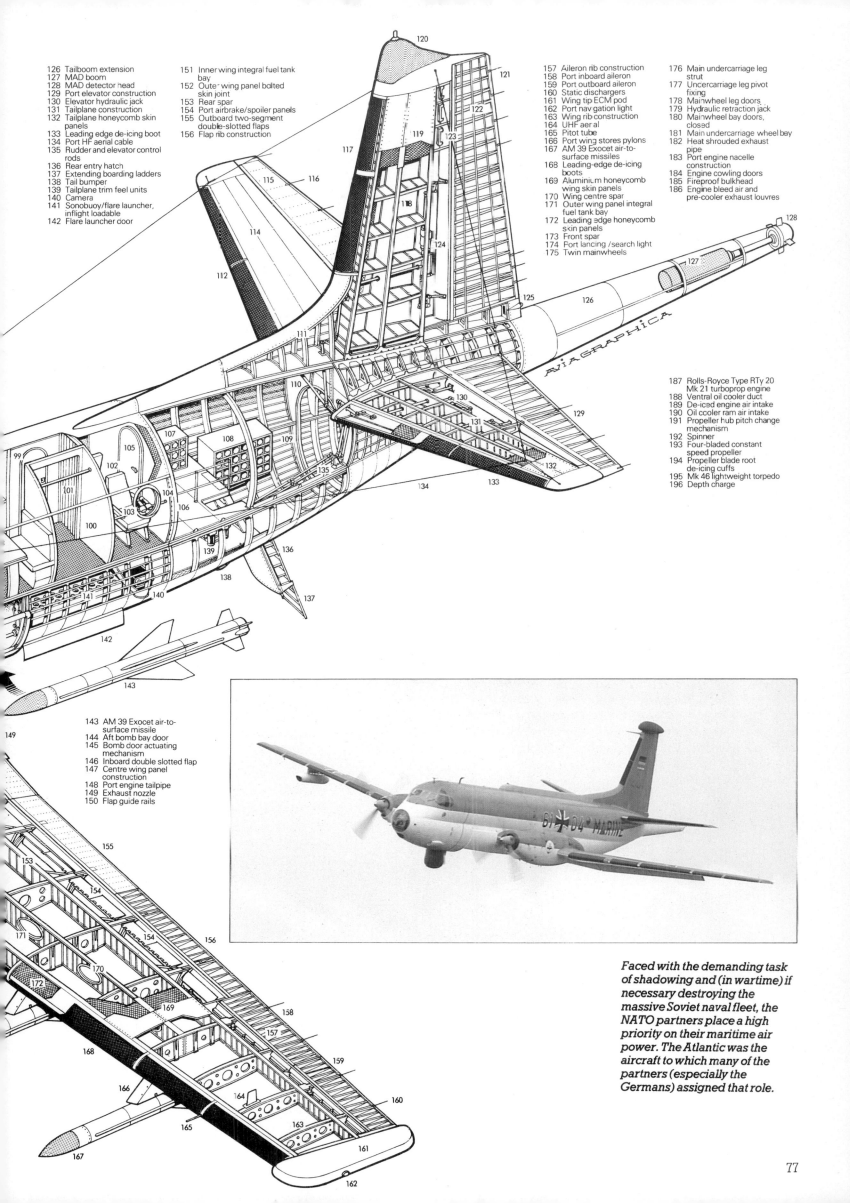

126 Tailboom extension
127 MAD boom
128 MAD detector head
129 Port elevator construction
130 Elevator hydraulic jack
131 Tailplane construction
132 Tailplane honeycomb skin panels
133 Leading edge de-icing boot
134 Port HF aerial cable
135 Rudder and elevator control rods
136 Rear entry hatch
137 Extending boarding ladders
138 Tail bumper
139 Tailplane trim feel units
140 Camera
141 Sonobuoy/flare launcher, inflight loadable
142 Flare launcher door

151 Inner wing integral fuel tank bay
152 Outer wing panel bolted skin joint
153 Rear spar
154 Port airbrake/spoiler panels
155 Outboard two-segment double-slotted flaps
156 Flap rib construction

157 Aileron rib construction
158 Port inboard aileron
159 Port outboard aileron
160 Static dischargers
161 Wing tip ECM pod
162 Port navigation light
163 Wing rib construction
164 UHF aerial
165 Pitot tube
166 Port wing stores pylons
167 AM 39 Exocet air-to-surface missiles
168 Leading-edge de-icing boots
169 Aluminium honeycomb wing skin panels
170 Wing centre spar
171 Outer wing panel integral fuel tank bay
172 Leading edge honeycomb skin panels
173 Front spar
174 Port landing /search light
175 Twin mainwheels

176 Main undercarriage leg strut
177 Undercarriage leg pivot fixing
178 Mainwheel leg doors
179 Hydraulic retraction jack
180 Mainwheel bay doors, closed
181 Main undercarriage wheel bay
182 Heat shrouded exhaust pipe
183 Port engine nacelle construction
184 Engine cowling doors
185 Fireproof bulkhead
186 Engine bleed air and pre-cooler exhaust louvres

187 Rolls-Royce Type RTy 20 Mk 21 turboprop engine
188 Ventral oil cooler duct
189 De-iced engine air intake
190 Oil cooler ram air intake
191 Propeller hub pitch change mechanism
192 Spinner
193 Four-bladed constant speed propeller
194 Propeller blade root de-icing cuffs
195 Mk 46 lightweight torpedo
196 Depth charge

143 AM 39 Exocet air-to-surface missile
144 Aft bomb bay door
145 Bomb door actuating mechanism
146 Inboard double slotted flap
147 Centre wing panel construction
148 Port engine tailpipe
149 Exhaust nozzle
150 Flap guide rails

Faced with the demanding task of shadowing and (in wartime) if necessary destroying the massive Soviet naval fleet, the NATO partners place a high priority on their maritime air power. The Atlantic was the aircraft to which many of the partners (especially the Germans) assigned that role.

British and European Combat Aircraft

The Franco-German Transall C.160 tactical transport is represented by an aircraft of Lufttransportgeschwader 62 at Wunsdorf, one of three German wings equipped with the type. Three production lines (two of them in Germany) built 169 first-generation aircraft for France, Germany and South Africa as the C.160F, C.160D and C.160Z respectively.

The Transall C.160 has recently been updated, including a refuelling probe mounted above the cockpit. The new generation Transall first flew at Aérospatiale's factory at Toulouse on 9 April 1981.

France is also producing a 'G2' version of the Transall C.160, a tactical transport built in collaboration with West Germany. The first of nine prototypes flew on 25 February 1963, and production aircraft were supplied to the Luftwaffe (110, including 20 transferred to Turkey), the French air force (50) and South Africa (nine), the last in March 1973. To meet a further French requirement for 28 transports and four airborne communications posts, an improved C.160 version was returned to production on the Aérospatiale line at Toulouse, and delivery was begun to the 64e Escadre de Transport (64th Transport Wing) at Evreux in December 1981. These new aircraft have an inflight-refuelling probe, and 10 also possess tanker capability through installation of a hose unit in the port landing gear pannier. Three civilian C.160s have been supplied to Indonesia and four fly on Air France's night postal service.

One of the more unusual international projects now under way is that for the Aeritalia-Aermacchi/EMBRAER AMX light strike fighter, which involves trans-Atlantic partnership between Italy and Brazil. The first of four European-built prototypes flew early in 1983, and a further two will be produced in South America before production deliveries late in 1986 against orders from Italy (187) and Brazil (79). Italy will use its aircraft to replace the Fiat G91R, G91T and Starfighter in eight squadrons (about half its front-line strength) but does not plan to acquire the proposed trainer version. Brazilian AMXs will supplant AT-26s.

The JuRom IAR-93A Orao is powered by two Rolls-Royce Viper 632 engines, licence-built in Bucharest. A further model, the IAR-93B, will have Viper 633s with afterburners.

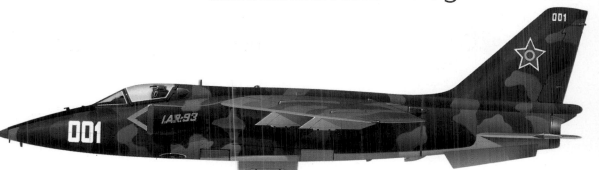

JuRom IAR-93A Orao of the Yugoslav air force. Assembled simultaneously at Mostar (Yugoslavia) and Craiova (Romania), the Orao is also built in tandem two-seat trainer version, the first of which flew in January 1977.

A second bi-national project is perhaps even more remarkable, in that the participants are on different sides of the Iron Curtain – although both are Communist countries. Romania (which is allowed unusual latitude by the Soviet Union and has built Western aircraft under licence) has joined forces with Yugoslavia, in the respective forms of their aircraft manufacturers CIAR and SOKO, to produce the JuRom IAR-93 Orao, a tactical fighter resembling the Jaguar or Mitsubishi F-1 from some angles. Flown in October 1974, the Orao is being built for the two countries' air arms and incorporates a significant number of British components, including two Viper engines. A pre-production batch of 15 aircraft, the first flying in 1978, was followed by series production a year later. The first delivery was in 1981 and orders for the Romanian air force total 185 Oraos, with a similar number believed to be destined for Yugoslavia. Developments include a two-seat trainer, and the IAR-93B, with afterburners.

American licence agreements

Any review of international projects must, of necessity, mention two US-designed aircraft built in considerable numbers by European manufacturers, and forming a significant proportion of NATO fighter-bomber strength. Production of the Lockheed F-104G Starfighter and its two-seat TF-104G trainer variant during the 1960s stemmed from the aircraft being chosen for a large-scale re-equipment programme in West Germany, and when other countries made similar decisions the scene was set for the establishment of four production centres (in Germany, Belgium, Italy and the Netherlands), whilst in addition Lockheed and Canadair fulfilled smaller orders from Denmark, Norway, Greece, Spain and Turkey. West Germany was the principal customer, its air force and navy operating 916 Starfighters for interceptor, strike and reconnaissance duties, and though branded as unsafe because of an initially high attrition rate the aircraft has subsequently proved to be no more unreliable than any other high-performance fighter of its era.

The Lockheed F-104S is the specially-developed version of the Starfighter built by Aeritalia, and some 205 have been delivered for service with nine gruppi of six Italian air force stormi.

Italy was unique in commissioning an advanced version of the aircraft to augment its F-104Gs,

British and European Combat Aircraft

By the early 1990s the entire front-line strength of the Netherlands air force will comprise General Dynamics F-16 Fighting Falcons in strike, interceptor and reconnaissance roles. In addition to wingtip Sidewinder air-to-air missiles, the aircraft may be equipped with a variety of ordnance on the wing pylons or an Orpheus recce pod beneath the fuselage.

and with an uprated engine, nine wing strongpoints and provision for Sparrow AAMs the resulting F-104S first flew in December 1966. Aeritalia built 246 of this version, including 40 for Turkey, and when the last was delivered in 1979 it was also the final Starfighter to be produced anywhere in the world.

With the exception of Turkey, the NATO nations are currently retiring their F-104G Starfighters, and four countries are now participating in a programme to build the General Dynamics F-16 Fighting Falcon in Europe by way of replacement. The exceptionally agile F-16A strike-interceptor and its F-16B trainer counterpart were selected by Belgium, Denmark, the Netherlands and Norway in 1975, plans calling for two assembly lines to be established. Fokker in the Netherlands was contracted to build aircraft for its own air force and Norway, whilst Avions Fairey-SABCA in Belgium had a similar arrangement with Denmark, but to offset purchase costs Danish and Norwegian aerospace companies received orders for several components and sub-assemblies to be incorporated in the completed aircraft.

The first 'Euro F-16' was a SABCA-assembled trainer flown on 11 December 1978, this also being the initial delivery, to the 349e Escadrille (349th Squadron) at Bevekom, on 26 January 1979. After the usual long working-up period with a new aircraft, the 349e Escadrille became the first European F-16 squadron to gain operational status, in January 1981. The Belgian air force now has 178 Fighting Falcons on order for complete re-equipment of its interceptor, strike and tactical reconnaissance units by the early 1990s. Denmark has 58 in process of delivery, its 727 Eskadrille (727th Squadron) accepting the first in January 1980.

From the Dutch production line, the 322nd Squadron received aircraft from July 1979 onwards, and Norway formed its 332nd Squadron at Rygge with the first of 72 F-16s in January 1980. Like Belgium, the Royal Netherlands air force will be entirely Falcon-equipped during the 1990s, from orders totalling 213.

Though Europe's smaller nations now find it financially convenient to build a ready-made design such as the F-16, a considerable potential for development of world-beating combat aircraft undoubtedly exists within the continent, its limiting factor being cash rather than capability. International collaborative design ventures will occupy an increasingly dominant sector of the European military (and civilian) aircraft scene in the years to come, and though conflicting national interests make difficult work of starting such projects, those now buying American may yet be persuaded to make even more broadly-based projects of the European combat aircraft to be designed in the future.

For those countries unable to afford the high cost of designing their own combat aircraft, licence production is a viable alternative. The first General Dynamics F-16 Fighting Falcon to be built in Europe for four NATO air forces was this Belgian F-16B trainer, FB-01, which made its initial flight on 11 December 1978.